Advance Praise for

DEAR FATHER

"J. Ivy is way more than a poet. He is a weaver of our fabric, a teller of our stories, a griot, an activist, a man. He has traveled the world fighting ignorance and injustice with his city on his back, the tears of his people in his pockets, and words as his weapons."

—**Talib Kweli**, hip-hop artist and activist

"J. Ivy has been blessed with a unique gift. He has the distinct ability to touch hearts and souls through the power of his voice, and to open eyes and minds through the truth of his words. I know that through this book, people who may be struggling with challenges will connect with his message and begin to experience their own healing."

—**Israel Idonije**, NFL veteran, humanitarian, and philanthropist

"I feel that J. Ivy is one of the most passionate, creative, and deep-thought–provoking poets to come in a very long time. I feel he is a very special spirit to give us so much insight and love and inspiration. He carries the blessing of our ancestors, and that gift in his words brings us light as we travel through these dark times. J. Ivy is light! God bless you my bro."

—**Doug E Fresh**, hip-hop legend and "The World's Greatest Entertainer"

"J. Ivy has always possessed the ability to communicate the social consciousness of this hip-hop generation. His work with Kanye West and others is revered globally. His 'Dear Father' poem touches me personally, being a son who didn't grow up with my father present in my life. What he articulates transcends economic and ethnic boundaries on many levels. Keep speaking, brother, the world needs healing."

—**Sway Calloway**, host of *The Wake Up Show*, producer, and MTV VJ

"I could say that J. Ivy has a way with words. I could say that he stands in a league of his own. I could say he's an amazing young talent—all of which, while being true, would be too obvious. It was all these things—delivery and the sound of his voice— that changed my perspective on his type of art. His voice in all facets of the word is simply legendary."

—**Estelle**, Grammy Award–winning singer/songwriter

"It's always a pleasure to work with someone who you can appreciate, someone who you respect, someone who you feel has talent, that can take us to the next level. J. Ivy is a healing poet, a brother who is concerned about the future of us."

—**Abiodun Oyewole** of The Last Poets

DEAR
FATHER

DEAR FATHER

BREAKING THE CYCLE OF PAIN

J. IVY

ATRIA BOOKS
New York London Toronto Sydney New Delhi

BEYOND WORDS
Hillsboro, Oregon

ATRIA BOOKS

A Division of Simon & Schuster, Inc.
1230 Avenue of the Americas
New York, NY 10020

BEYOND WORDS

20827 N.W. Cornell Road, Suite 500
Hillsboro, Oregon 97124-9808
503-531-8700 / 503-531-8773 fax
www.beyondword.com

Copyright © 2015 by James Ivy Richardson II

All rights reserved, including the right to reproduce this book or portions thereof in any form whatsoever without prior written permission. For information, address Atria Books/Beyond Words Subsidiary Rights Department, 1230 Avenue of the Americas, New York, NY 10020.

Managing editor: Lindsay S. Brown
Editors: Henry Covey, Emily Han
Copyeditor: Kristin Thiel
Proofreader: Mark Antonides
Design: Devon Smith
Cover photos: Andre' Wright, Jr
Composition: William H. Brunson Typography Services
Director of "Dream BIG": Chris Velona
Music Producer for "Dream BIG": Rich Sancho
Director of "I Need to Write": Cam Be
Director of "Dear Father": Coodie & Chike
Director of "Dear Father" trailer: Jamaar J.
Music Producer for "Dear Father" video: Aaron Richardson

First Atria Books/Beyond Words hardcover edition January 2015

ATRIA BOOKS and colophon are trademarks of Simon & Schuster, Inc. Beyond Words Publishing is an imprint of Simon & Schuster Inc., and the Beyond Words logo is a registered trademark of Beyond Words Publishing, Inc.

For more information about special discounts for bulk purchases, please contact Simon & Schuster Special Sales at 1-866-506-1949 or business@simonandschuster.com.

The Simon & Schuster Speakers Bureau can bring authors to your live event. For more information or to book an event, contact the Simon & Schuster Speakers Bureau at 1-866-248-3049 or visit our website at www.simonspeakers.com.

Manufactured in the United States of America

10 9 8 7 6 5 4 3 2 1

Library of Congress Cataloging-in-Publication Data

Ivy, J.,
    Dear father : breaking the cycle of pain / J. Ivy. — First Atria Books/Beyond Words hardcover edition.
        pages   cm
    1. Ivy, J., 1976–.   2. Poets, American—21st century—Biography.   3. Rap musicians—United States—Biography.   4. Chicago (Ill.)—Biography.   I. Title.
    PS3609.V94Z46   2015
    811'.6—dc23
    [B]

                                                                    2014024650

ISBN 978-1-58270-508-8
ISBN 978-1-4767-7825-9 (ebook)

The corporate mission of Beyond Words Publishing, Inc.: *Inspire to Integrity*

To

James Ivy Richardson Sr.,
My love for you, for my father, is genuine and true...

and

Pamela Richardson,
For the purity of your love, guidance, and strength...

I truly THANK GOD *for you both!*

CONTENTS

CONTENTS

Part II: Purpose

Part III: Power

CONTENTS

YOUR PAST CAN KILL YOUR FUTURE

If you don't deal with your emotions,
One day your emotions are going to deal with you.

How do you destroy what you cannot see? How do you protect yourself from attacks lurking in your blind spots? How do you stop an untouchable darkness from spreading in your soul?

These hidden issues that preyed on me, these problems that wrestled with my soul, there, in the midst of my subconscious, they grew beastly, feasting nightly on my misery, transforming my joy into my pain.

These emotional beasts were mean, angry, hurt, and abandoned. Hungry and vicious, they preyed on my every move, I had no clue when the next emotional attack was coming—I was lost in this jungle of my own fears.

I struggled with this pain. It became a constant member of my life, finding ways to maneuver around my emotional defenses and crushing the foundation of my spirit. I felt confused, undervalued, and lonely. My confidence was shattered. I didn't know who I was. I didn't know what gifts I possessed.

Look, I'm not the manic depressed person singing,
"Woe is me"
in a not-so-perfect key, looking for
someone's sympathy.
I confess! That's just not me. It's not my
makeup or part of my personality.

But at different points in my life, I have found myself haunted. I never played the victim, but I was victimized, tormented, hypnotized by the lies that my doubts told me. As a child I struggled with feeling worthy. Namely, I felt like I wasn't good enough for my dad.

This shifted my entire psyche, extending to every facet of my life. My confidence was compromised—my edge was dulled 'cause I was not being challenged by the leader of my home team. My passion was limited 'cause I was not charged by the energy of a parent's love. Similar to the markings left behind by lightning striking delicate earth, I was scarred with a permanent pain, a constant reminder of my reality. My father had left me.

What did I do to deserve this? These feelings. *These feelings?* These spells of depression. You have no idea how heavy this pain can be. Or maybe you do? Maybe, just maybe, you've swam these drowning waters before, choking on fear, anchored, weighed down, held back by a disloyalty to take care of yourself, circled by the sharks of your past, which cut their teeth into the unloving layers that you thought you left behind.

I walk around
With God's jumper cables
Clamped

To

My

Soul,
Gripping my spirit,
Jolting
My existence . . .
1—2—3

CLEAR!

I'm clear when I'm there . . .
When I'm here . . .
In a cloudless sky,
I can see again.

Inside I was off balance. I was unaware of the deep, dark hole that rested beneath my heels. I was down. Life had punted away my will, and those newly developed beasts headquartered in the shadows of my lower self kept pushing me into the depths of my hell, time and time again. Who could I call for help? Who would hear my cries of despair? Who?

My saving grace was my pen and my poetry, my voice.

At a young age, I was shown that I had a tool that would allow me to build ladders out of any pit of pain. Being blessed with this tool was a gift. Over time I would learn how to use this gift that would empower me to write—and right—my wrongs. I would follow my instinctive guide with passion, belief, and an internal strength to climb and focus my eyes toward a healthy future.

They say that the sky's the limit, but I now believe that space is the limit, and space is limitless. I now realize that we all have been equipped with gifts that can help us build ladders out of our pain. As a superbly creative species, there isn't anything that we are incapable of doing. When worlds are destroyed, we have the beautiful ability and the undying will to build again. We fall, but we get back up. We break down, but we heal again. Again . . .

If you don't deal with your emotions,
One day your emotions are going to deal with you.

I knew that it was time for me to take control of the internal steering wheel that misguided me on this path. I realized it was time for me to go back to the pen and find myself.

DREAM BIG
True, life may seem at an all-time low:
You've tried everything,
But you can't seem to find your flow,
So success comes slow and problems tend to grow.
You've seen your friends shine like its 100°,
> While you chillin' at 10 below.
It's cold out here,
> It's freezing,
The bad times are increasing.
Bad energy is all that your surroundings are releasing,
So misery's been feasting on your soul.
Vices grab hold,
And loads get **heavy**,
You feel so **HEAVY**.
But you can't **BLOCK**

              your blessings
When they come your way,
You got to be ready,
Ready to receive.
You got to shake off the fear and believe.
'Cause at times we're tested,
Tested to see how STRONG we really are,
How far we'll really go.
There's an army GROWING,
But you can't join unless you know what you're fighting for,
'Cause if you stand for nothing,
You'll f
        a
          l
            l
               for anything.
So stand T
         A
         L
         L,
Know that you can't walk until you crawl,
You can't run until you walk,
You can't fly without a running start.
So pump your arms when you come off the blocks,
And it won't do you no harm to come off your block,
Get out and see the world,
'Cause everyone has their own mountain top,
It wasn't promised to a few,
But promised to those who knew.
So climb the way you breathe and never stop,
                                Inhale your best,

Exhale the BS.

Keep on keepin' on.

See where you're going and work on getting there.

Don't hate on others when others get theirs,

'Cause you go' get yours.

You go knock down your own doors,

Know that GOD go take care of you and yours.

That's why miracles happen out of the blue,

So know that and remember that can't nobody stop you but YOU,

'Cause Dreams Don't Come True,

They Are True,

So Dream Big!

Then after that,

Dream even **Bigger!!**

So **BIG** that Martin and Coretta are up in heaven holding hands,

Smiling down on us,

With a tear in their eyes,

And joy in their hearts,

Saying,

"Amen . . .

Amen . . .

Amen!"

 Live performance of Dream BIG
http://tagr.com/t/V4cJRV

PART I

PAIN

I WISH YOU COULD HAVE BEEN THERE THE 1ST TIME I SANG!
I WISH YOU COULD HAVE SEEN HOW YO BABY BOY FLOW!
I WISH YOU COULD HAVE SEEN ME ROCK JUST ONE SHOW

I WISH SO
DEARLY THAT YOU DIDN'T
HAVE TO GO, TO GO.

DEAR FATHER

WHON

DEAR FATHER,   YOU KNOW I DON'T HAVE MANY REGRETS   I'VE BEEN
                                        HOW YOU'VE   REFLECTIO

* THIS MAY HURT BUT I GOT TO WRITE THIS LETTER
HEART BROKEN   YOU WERE A MAJOR INFL
        MAYBE ILL FEEL BETTER

IM SORRY I NEVER BOTHERED TO WRITE YOU BEFORE. BUT
THERE WAS NEVER A NEED CAUSE I JUST KNEW YOU CO
RUNNING
WALKING BACK THROUGH THAT DOOR. I EVEN LEFT IT AS
                        WITH SO MUCH LOVE IN E
YOU SAID I WAS THE CENTER OF YOUR UNIVERSE SO I KNEW YO
ME. I MEAN WHATS A MAN WITHOUT HIS CORE. WHATS
FATHER WITHOUT HIS BABY BOY. PERHAPS LIKE A CHILD WIT
TOY. (I) OR A CHILD WITH NO JOY.

DEAR DAD,   HARD TO   MISLED   I MISS YOU   TIME HEA
              WRITE FEEL OUT OF WHAK   SICK IN THA HEAD   EVERYTHING

I WAS SUPPOSE TO BE WRITIN A POEM, BUT I FIGURED
I WOULD WRITE YOU INSTEAD. YOU'VE BEEN ON MY MIND ALOT LATELY
                    SEEM TO
MEAN I CANT GET YOU OUT MY HEAD. MENTALLY I FEEL D
DEAR DAD,   SOUL SOILED   FRANTIC
        IM WRITIN BECAUSE
IF SOMEONE WHY IM WRITIN IM NOT FOR CERTAIN. MAYBE
BECAUSE IF SOMEONE OPENED MY SOULS CERTAIN THEY WOULD
THAT IM HURTIN. WHY MAYBE ITS BECAUSE YOU WERE SUPPOSE
BE HERE FOREVER. AND WHY YOU WERE HERE WE WERE SUPP
TO BE TOGETHER. BUT INSTEAD IT WAS WHATEVER. TIME WA
TAKEN FOR GRANITE. MY SKY IS FALLING BUT OUTKAST SAID
ME NO NEED TO PANIC. VISIONS NOW COME IN PANORAMIC
DEAR DAD,
THESE WORDS ARE BEING WRITTEN AND SPOKEN BECAU
HEART BROKEN. NEW BEGUN WORLD IM IN PAIN
I STILL HAVENT HEARD AFTER ALL OF YOU GOT ME OPEN HOPIN THIS ILL FEELING WIL
I WEAR A MASK SO MY PEEPS WO
WONT

HOME SWEET HOME, CHICAGO

As a child, I was lost in my fantasies, having fun finding my way. I was innocent and naïve to life's pressures and vice grips. I was a kid with no worries, a lil black boy who some said looked like little Michael Jackson. Once, when comedian Damon Williams saw an old picture of me in one of my poetry books, he joked that I looked like a member of the Jackson 6. Maybe it was the Afro? (Thank God I never had a Jheri Curl.)

Our middle-class family didn't have all the riches in the world, but we had each other, and we had Chicago. The Chi is a very proud city of hardworking, hustling, good-hearted people, a town founded by a Haitian black man named Jean Baptiste Point du Sable. It is the home of our beloved first elected black mayor, Harold Washington, whose sudden passing in 1987 shook the city to its core. It is home to the infamous Al Capone, Jeff Fort, and Larry Hoover. It was the launching point for Mahalia Jackson and Nat King Cole. It's the home of

Muddy Waters; Curtis Mayfield; Gwendolyn Brooks; Harrison Ford; Carl Sandburg; Earth, Wind & Fire; Chaka Khan; Bernie Mac; and Lou Rawls. It is the birthplace of Donny Hathaway, Gil Scott-Heron, Quincy Jones, Don Cornelius, and *Soul Train*. It's home to the blues and the lounges that housed it. House music (RIP, Frankie Knuckles, the godfather of house music) and steppin' were both born within the boundaries of this great town. The rhythm of those Chicago winds has forever dictated our moves, art, music, and conversation. It's as if our words dance when we talk. Our walk is accompanied by a confident glide. The city's movement, its essence, pulsates within us and around us, waiting to be beautifully translated by its creative citizens. This energy that guides us is as tribal as what guided the tribes we were snatched from. No, it hasn't been easy, but because of our hope for better days, we have managed to make our way.

I grew up on the South Side, Eighty-Seventh and Winchester, the corner of the hood, the edge of darkness, the black belt that was fastened together by love and separated from the rest of society by expressways and major intersections. It was our piece of the hyper-segregated pie. You just didn't see white folks in our hood. From the mailman and the Jehovah's Witnesses who knocked on the door to the grocery store clerks and the teachers, we revolved thru life in our black bubble. Cops stalked our neighborhoods, and trouble lurked in the alleys we played in, but we didn't live in fear. We lived by making it day to day. My grandfather would always say, "If you can make it in Chicago, you can make it anywhere—just keep on keepin' on. Take it one day at a time."

And that's what we did: we kept moving forward. Innocent blue-collar workers and ruthless gangstas walked together on the tight streets that boxed us in, still searching for the pride that slavery stole. Tribes formed after we swarmed from the South, descendants of slaves and sharecroppers, folks who wanted nothing more than a fair shake at life. We traded dirt roads for asphalt, wooden houses for concrete buildings, crops for factories and steel mills. Most black parents, who were born during the baby boom, worked hard providing for their families, believing their children's way out of the hood required us going to school and getting a good job. Often they would preach, "In this white world, you have to be twice as good just to get a chance." Without putting this thought into context, we could have easily deemed ourselves as not being smart or good enough for society, but as I got older, I realized they were simply trying to say that advances were limited for blacks. There were only so many good business and trade jobs, only so many recording contracts, the NFL and NBA only had so many spots, and college was far from free.

What were your options? Go to school or the school of hard knocks? Do you head for college or down the quick road to jail? Many didn't see a way out so they hustled and encouraged you to do the same. Gangster Disciples (GDs), Black Disciples (BDs), Vice Lords, Four Corner Hustlers, and Black Stones patrolled and ruled the streets more than the cops did. The cats pushing the fancy cars with big rims and loud music were our role models. The smart kids, the nerds, were considered lame. Emotions and egos were tugged on. Pulled on. Pushed. Kids walked to school but wouldn't walk back. Some were snatched up by strangers in vans. Friends got caught in the crossfire of the war zone we dwelled in; others were picked up by the cops and introduced to the system. Some were jumped into gangs. Forced to slang. Forced to do things their hearts didn't intend.

What do you want to be when you grow up? I never heard "a killer." I never heard "hustler," "pimp," or "drug dealer." I never heard "basement dweller." But I heard my moms when she would say, "If you go to jail, don't expect me to come visit you." I heard her loud and clear when she lectured me and my older brother as she drove us down Roosevelt Avenue, where the buildings were run-down and tatted with gang signs, the sidewalks were decorated with broken glass, the trash blew thru like tumbleweed, and the air smelled like urine and crack. She showed us blocks of drunks, addicts, and homeless folks and said, "If you don't go to school and get an education, this is where you go' end up." You can't help but hear that.

Sirens SCREAMED like alarm clocks.
The struggle unlocked the inner beast.
Some worked,
Some worked the streets,
Our blocks that were occupied by common folk . . .
Bus drivers, mailmen, gangstas,
And corner dwellers,
Who I would walk past in a worn-out sweater,
Rocking a nappy shag,
While they sipped brown liquor out of brown paper bags . . .
The pusher man pushed that white for the fiends,
Red and Blue gangs terrorized the black scene,
The older kids smoked that green.
                        Stress is a hell of a drug.
Daily, the stress of the city tried killing our love,
Tried suffocating our flow . . .
If there's a HELL BELOW,
It made its way up to our bungalows and two-flats,
The gangways and alleys,
Yea, though I walk thru the shadow of the valley
of crime sprees,
You see,
We feared the evils that stalked us.
"Boy, did you lock the doors?"
Security became yet another chore,

Because we dwelled where purses got snatched,
Where older women and young girls were attacked,
Where folks were carjacked,
Where cats were pistol-whipped and hit with bats . . .

"MAN, YOU KNOW WHERE YOU AT?!
YOU BETTER STRAIGHTEN THAT HAT!"

I never understood that,
I never understood the fights,
Because the blocks looked peaceful on sight.
Our folks taught us how to work hard and do what's right.
We celebrated life at the cookouts,
Soul music whistled thru the nights.
At the same time,
Black men were ushered off in cuffs, screaming,

"I KNOW MY RIGHTS!"

I guess that's why I had to be in before the streetlights came on.
Ma just wanted to make sure her boys came home and had a chance
    to grow,
Praying that we weren't swallowed up by this place the Natives called
    Checagou,
Land of smelly air . . .
There,
Here,
The air smelled of exhaust and evergreen trees,
Cookie factories and steel mills,
Cigarette smoke and barbecued ribs.
Life seemed so simple as a kid,

Bag lunches, cartoons, and curfews.
But I slowly found out how much these streets will hurt you,
    Murk you,
        Choke you,
           Shoot you,
              Loot you,
Put its boot to yo' neck and beat you,
Cheat you,
Clown you,
Drown you in the cracks of the asphalt.
We fought,
Over the invisible borders of our town.
Rarely did we go downtown.
I guess the racial tension was just TOO THICK.
Maybe we were all just too sick,
Too tired,
Too mixed up in the head to move ahead as a people.
So in our piece,
        Of the piece,
           Of the piece of the pie,
We sat by in our sections of the city feeling inadequate and unequal,

Boxed in by political maps,

Mentally trapped.
Bank accounts were damn near tapped but we counted our blessings,
Pressed our luck.
Like the grilled cheese on the roof of my mouth, we were stuck,
But like any kid did . . .
I peddled my red and yellow Big Wheel,
Simply waiting on the melody of the ice cream truck . . .

My two brothers (Virgil and Sergio) and I were raised by my moms to not give up, but many of our good friends did give. Many gave in to influence. Birds of a feather usually nest together. You become a product of your environment, guilty by association, mimicking the wrong movements. I was associated with good folks who made bad decisions. Choices paint our paths, and most of these childhood roads had dead ends with dead bodies rotting in the shadows of abandoned buildings. My moms watched some of her brothers take the corner hustle route, and she didn't want that for us.

Not her boys, her gifts. She wanted us to find that proper chance, so she tried her best to shelter us from the streets. She paid us for good grades and punished us for bad ones. She challenged us. Made us work for everything, cleaning up the house, busting suds til the hot water mysteriously crinkled the skin on our fingers, walking the dog when we didn't feel like it, plucking weeds til calluses bloomed on our hands, barreling pounds of dirt, and cutting down small trees. After we waxed the floors, we would run and slide on them in our colorful striped tube socks that we kept pulled up to our knees. We had fun, but we put in work—and our wage was minimum. Moms called it an allowance, but this kind of money wouldn't allow us to grow.

I did anything to have some cash for the trips to the mall, 'cause I was tired of wearing hand-me-down sweaters. I hated when my moms bought me those hard Buster Brown shoes to correct my crooked feet. When times were tight, she got us Pro Wings from Payless Shoe-Source and our blue jeans from Sears. Mine were always slims. My older brother, Virgil, wore huskies. We couldn't stand our clothes, and we made sure to complain about it, but on cue Moms would always say, "Boy, you better be rich, 'cause you got rich taste buds."

On the outside my clothes were busted until I got older, but in my mind I always had flavor and style. First impressions were everything.

It determined how people respected you. It showed how cool you were. It shaped folks' opinions when they talked about you. You had to coordinate. What you wore became your voice, a reflection of your personality. Whether your reflection was bold, modest, flashy, bummy, or smooth, we wore our emotions on our sleeves . . . literally. Just another part of the Chicago way.

SEARCHING FOR FREEDOM

I was two years old the first time I rode a bike with no training wheels. Yes, two! All right, closer to two and a half, but that's still amazing, if you ask me. I was always very tall for my age. I was five-foot-five in the third grade. Up until fourth grade, I was the tallest kid in the class. I was six-foot-one my freshman year of high school, and I just knew I was going to end up hitting six-foot-four or six-foot-five. Point being, when I was two, I had the height of a four or five year old when my parents decided to buy me what I referred to as kid's gold, my little orange bike.

Now, once a kid gets up, running, and moving, there's nothing better than learning to get rolling. And that's exactly what I did! I loved my bike. The Big Wheel was cool, but the bike was better. Like most kids my age, I was challenged by the art of balance, so my parents eliminated my fear and secured my fun by attaching training wheels to my imaginary motorcycle. *Zoom!* If the weather was nice enough to be outside, I was either already out there on my bike or inside begging my parents to let me go out.

One day my father snatched the training wheels off of my bike.

"No!" I yelled, thinking my fun had been sidelined.

My dad didn't see it that way. "Boy, you're too big for training wheels," he said, looking at his little, tall son.

Being too young to rationalize what was happening, I ran into the house mad and crying to my Moms, telling her what Dad had done. She looked at me with that sweet motherly pity and said, "There ain't nothing that I can do about it."

Frustrated with both of my parents, I went back out.

When I hit the yard, my dad waved for me to come to where he stood in the shade of the big evergreen tree at the top of the gangway, holding the bike upright by its seat. In Chicago, what we call a gangway drapes every house. A gangway is a small sidewalk that stretches from the alley, thru the backyard, alongside the house, to the sidewalk out front. Ours was slightly slanted.

When I finally reached my giant of a father, he kindly told me to get on. Not daring to disobey him, I reluctantly straddled the bike, putting my feet on the pedals, with my focus fixed on finding my new balance. Once I somewhat steadied myself, he asked if I was ready. I hesitantly nodded yes, and then he pushed me away!

Terrified, I quickly glided down the gangway thru the backyard, alongside our house. When I reached the end of the gangway out front, I turned right onto the sidewalk and instinctively started peddling. No longer filled with anger and anxiety, instead overwhelmed with pure joy and unconscious of this moment's significance, I freely flew down the block, passing house after house after house . . .

I was two years old

DEAR FATHER

riding my little orange bike
without any training wheels!

Wow!

He pushed me out into the world,
And so began my search for freedom,
My escape from the chains that I've chosen,
That chose me,
The prisons that posture in my mind.
My people gallop in the quicksand of struggle,
We huddle in misery,
Our smiles are rudely interrupted,
Habits become linked to our history.
I'm choking on secondhand answers,
But as a little boy my grandmother taught me to have pride in the
    visions I see,
My mother advises me to be free.
I talk back thru the glass,
Petition thru the partition,
Our hands touch different sides of the window,
As I beg GOD for the key...
The keys to life are too heavy for this janitor's belt,
I have to lighten the load to properly clean.
Can't do that when the load is too heavy for the washing machine,
When dreams are deferred,
Becoming mean is preferred.
I'm angered by the dangers of self.
I'm trying to shake it off,
'Cause I don't know how many days are left.
I write timelines with every step.

Every breath is a chance,
To strap on my wings,
Surf the breeze,
Freeze my pain,
Thaw out my joy that's been froze like a cold pose,
Stand out like a bold rose . . .
Bright,
Smooth,
Rigid,
Regarded by the angels in the stands,
I can hear their cheers.
I use these precious years,
To escape the clutches of my fears,
Run naked,
Shielded by vulnerability,
Gripping on to the energy of my ability,
Striking with rhythm I stand on mine,
I post up religiously,
Open the doors of my chivalry,
War with my handicaps,
Spawn my delivery,
I see it so vividly,
As I use my future to write my history,
Use my history to rebuild my kingdom,
As I look for,
Fight for,
Search for . . .
My Freedom.

DJ JIM RICHARDS

June 5, 1984

WVON: News While It's News

In the news at this hour, an FBI mole who posed as a crooked attorney has testified that he won four favorable rulings after passing some $1,200 thru middle men to a judge...

Police say they still don't know who's responsible for the pipe bombs that have started appearing in Chicago. Yesterday for the third time in five days, a pipe bomb similar to those discovered in Wisconsin and Minnesota was found in Chicago...

Authorities also say a Chicago police officer was wounded and a twenty-two-year-old South Side man killed late last night in a shootout...

And in sports, the Cubs have the day off. The Sox
6, the Angels 4. The Sox will play California again
tonight at Comiskey Park, and the Cubs are at Mon-
treal in an evening game...
For WVON, I'm Jim Richards.

My father, James Ivy Richardson Sr., was a former Air Force veteran who returned to Chicago in 1962 after four years of service and an honorable discharge. He worked as a bus driver for the Chicago Transit Authority (CTA), but his true desire was to become a radio personality and DJ. And that's what he eventually did. From the mid 1970s thru the late 1980s, my dad, aka Jim Richards, worked in several markets around the country. In the early 80s he landed a job on the most popular black station in Chicago, at the time, WVON 1450 AM. In the mornings, if you were at home watching television, this young lady named Oprah Winfrey was hosting a show called *AM Chicago*, and if you were in your car commuting to work, you may have been listening to my dad on WVON.

Standing in the living room by the wood-grained floor-model radio, I listened to him before I walked to school. As a young child, though Dad broadcasting to millions of people was the norm, I still found it amazing to hear my dad's voice stream out of the speakers. His voice was distinctive, warm, smooth, and strong. It was immaculate. You couldn't help but listen and be mesmerized. Quite like a great preacher's tone, the depth of Barry White's bravado, or the magnetism of James Earl Jones' Darth Vader performance, Dad's voice was demanding of your time. It was so powerful, you could feel it in your core when he spoke—and as someone who knew him off the radio, I also knew it had the power to shake the house when he got mad.

I stood there like a stone,

SOLID,
Still,
Feet planted on the hardwood,
Rooted by a voice that stemmed thru the air.
My family tree was branching out from the radio in front of me,
Streaming a transmission that was quickly caught by rabbit ears,
Antennas that translated the familiar frequency, hopping thru my
    heart,
This was a voice I knew . . .
It was the same voice that told me happy birthday,
The same voice that told me to do my homework,
The same voice that told me to go outside and play.
This station had me at attention,
Staring at the amplifier,
Counting the numbers on the dial,
Rationalizing the science inside,
Hypnotized by the magic that captured my familiarity.
How did Dad get in there?
How did he get inside of the radio?

The mystique and personality of the DJ was such a big part of our
lives, impacting our days, our moods, and our outlooks, especially
during a time when the black community was underrepresented in
the world of media. Yes, we had *Soul Train*; we had *Jet* and *Ebony*
magazines, which were often collector's items in black households;
and we had the occasional television show like *Sanford and Son*,
What's Happening!!, *Good Times*, *The Jeffersons*, *The Cosby Show*,
and *A Different World*, but overall you didn't often see a reflection
of yourself on television, in major films, or in magazines. So it was
a big deal for my family whenever my dad's voice would pour out of
the radio.

By the time I got up; by the time I ate my grits, eggs, Cream of Wheat, Corn Flakes, Trix, Chex, Rice Krispies, Cheerios, or oatmeal; by the time I grabbed my Pac-Man lunch box equipped with a bologna sandwich and Thermos filled with red Kool-Aid, picked up my homework, my Mead folders, and packed up my book bag, so I could walk to school with my brother, Virgil, my dad had already been gone most of the morning, taking off in the middle of the night to relieve the night DJ and prep for his show.

He had the hip-1970s-blaxploitation style to go with his voice. He didn't dress exactly like a pimp, but his style was pimpish-cool. He had a swagger, an undeniable confidence that was evident when he walked in the room in his polished hard shoes. He was always booted, suited in the latest fashion: slim slacks, patterned shirts, turtlenecks, blue jeans jackets, and leather coats. He curled his mustache to perfection, which brought attention to the majesty of his skin and the deepness of his eyes. He had the traditional Richardson nose: curved, bold, and unique. He was handsome like your favorite star. He looked like one of the lead actors in *Super Fly*.

One of my older cousins on my dad's side once told me, "Jimmy, if a thousand men walked past with paper bags on their heads, you would know which one your dad was 'cause of his walk! His walk was mean, man! It was a stroll. Almost like he was gliding . . . and when he spoke, everyone listened!"

My aunt Christine, the second born of my father's two older siblings, would always tell me how caring and giving he was. She said he was very compassionate and very protective. She said he had a huge heart. Whether he was helping someone work on their car or taking Virgil and me bike riding, folks loved his company. When family called for help, he was there—his care for others shined through.

What I saw was a young Mississippi man who was fun and happy, his laugh contagious. He took care of my moms and his boys. He drove a cool brown AMC Hornet with tan stripes racing down its sides. He smoked packs of squares a day, and his drink of choice was Old Style beer and dark liquor. He was good at making things. He loved putting together model motorized cars and planes, which he would drive and fly for the kids on the block to admire. He had a huge train set complete with toy people, trees, and streetlights, with the train chugging along tracks that ran on for miniature miles.

When he wasn't happy, he would lie on the couch in the basement and watch television. I don't remember him saying, "I love you," when I was young, but he showed it by cooking us Malt-O-Meal or pork and beans. He showed it thru his smile when he would take us to fly kites, and when he would sing me happy birthday. Or when he would surprise me and pop up at my school to see how I was doing in class. I felt the love when I would drive around the city with him and being proudly introduced as his son Jimmy.

I know the cool, charismatic man I call Dad was a good man. I believe that's the quality that drew people to him—the quality that pushed my grandmother to encourage my moms to date him in the first place. That's the quality that magnetized him to conversations with the neighbors on the block, the quality that put smiles on the faces of family and friends.

To this day, my moms still lights up when she talks about the good times. She said he was funny and fun to be around. Said he was silly. The last time we talked about him, she started to laugh, which always warms my heart, then told me about this time when they were down in his home state of Mississippi. "So here we are driving down this lil dirt road, and James sees a rabbit. This fool pulls the car over and starts chasing the rabbit around in the field. Cracked me up!"

My moms really loved my dad, and he really loved her. I know they did. I know they still do. I remember the laughs. I remember the stories my mother would tell me about my dad playing the saxophone.

I remember the stories of them going bowling and riding on my dad's motorcycle. I remember hearing about the card parties. I remember being at the card parties. I remember the story of him rushing from the radio station (WMPP 1470 AM) he was working for way out in Chicago Heights, picking up my in-labor mother, and trying to dodge the pot-holes that triggered her anguish and contractions as they sped to the University of Chicago where I was born, moments after their arrival, that third day of March. I remember their warm feelings. And you can see that warmth and love in old pictures of them together. You can hear it in my moms' voice. This was her man, her husband, the biological father of two of her sons, and the dad to her oldest son. He was the person she leaned on for protection. He was her heart. And she was his.

MA, GOODNESS

My mother isn't and has never been the one you could run over. She's a South Side girl, the fourth child of seven. Growing up in Chicago during the civil rights movement, she's known segregation and desegregation. From her upbringing thru her romantic relationships, from Chicago politics and racism to the demands of her job as a registered nurse, she's experienced enough to write her own book.

Her intuition makes her wiser than most. She knows what she knows, and lets you know exactly how she feels. She can't help it. It's in her nature. Honesty spills out of her. When I was younger, it went in one ear and out the other. When I got a little older and she shelled out her advice, I knew she was right most of the time, so now I do listen. I'm so appreciative of her words, but I can't let her have all the fun. When she gets into one of her zones and rattles off her thoughts, instead of responding with an aggravated "my goodness," I keep things fun and tease her by following up her statements, concerns, and wise suggestions with a "Ma, goodness . . ." That always makes her laugh.

For years my mother worked at Cook County Hospital, inspiration for the hospital in the television show *ER*, and then she supervised a clinic for diabetics called the West Suburban Dialysis Center (South Side Unit). After visiting her at work a few times and seeing how much she helped people, how many people she helped, and how she held people's lives in her hands, I can only imagine the weight she had to carry over the years. Every day she witnessed folks hooked up to machines battling thru blood transfusions, taking meds, tired, exhausted, fighting for their lives, and every day she helped them fight. My mother has a *huge* heart, so I know she absorbed and endured a lot.

She's sweet, but tough. She's the rose you don't want to grab the wrong way. Even though she would let me hop in the bed with her and my dad, shielding me from my nightmares, she urged me to fight my fears. Yeah, she would hold me tight during those thunderstorms, but she wasn't a coddler. When times got hard and I shot her threats of running away, she would quickly say, "Go ahead. What are you waiting on? You think I'm treating you bad? Get out there and see how bad those streets treat you." Quickly I would change my mind. Her goal was to make my two brothers and me better, and her way of doing that was with tough love. So when we got mad and said we were going to call the police, she would say, "There's the phone. Call the cops and see what happens to you."

Raising three boys in Chicago, she was exactly what she had to be. She knew that life and the streets we had to walk would swallow us up if we didn't have the right guidance, so she let us know who was boss, and we respected her authority. We respected her ideals, her rules, her wisdom, her intelligence, her presence, and the look in her eyes, be it filled with a soft, gentle love or "boy, don't play with me!"

Like most black women, she truly was a superwoman. She could pull off anything once she put her mind to it. I remember this one time when my moms, Virgil, and I were driving home down Ashland Avenue in her orange, beat-up, two-door AMC Gremlin. Due to the backseat floor being rusted out, we were all cramped tight in the front seat. It was so bad, whenever we did ride in the back, we had to keep our feet up to avoid the speedy pavement below.

When we hit Eighty-Seventh Street, we made a right turn at the convenience store Pot of Gold, where people in the neighborhood bought things like bread, cleaning supplies, and lottery tickets. I would always stare up at the store's giant, colorful sign, happily entranced by the fluorescent coins piling up in the big pot. I daydreamed about that treasure in the sky being mine, so I could give it to my folks. I wanted to take care of them. It was my wish, my leprechaun dream. But seeing it also meant home was near.

As we turned the corner, and I continued staring up at the sign, the passenger door suddenly flew open! Sitting the closest to the door, I started falling toward a fatal end. Looking down at the littered asphalt, my eyes had a growth spurt, my heart jumped out of my chest. I was scared out of my mind. I was going to be a victim to gravity and bad timing. With it happening so fast, I didn't know what to do. What could I do? I couldn't fly, I couldn't reverse the laws of nature, but in one superhero motion, my mother reached over Virgil, grabbed my arm, snatched me back into that rusted car, and closed the door all while successfully completing the turn.

That's how my life with my mother has been. She's had one hand on the wheel of life with her other hand reaching out to us, holding us, doing her best to pull us out of harm's way. Life keeps on moving, and she moves with it; she lives by her words and "keeps on trucking," adapting to her new chapters, refusing to give up on the challenges of life. Her adventurous spirit inspires me to live boldly.

She's the strongest woman I've ever seen or ever known. She's super-human. She's genuine. She's a great person. I'm proud of her, proud to be her son, proud to call her Ma.

EVERY DAY IS MOTHER'S DAY

Ma, EVERY day I celebrate YOU,
Because your love has NO limit,
No blemish.
I celebrate your natural willingness to care and encourage,
I admire your courage and strength.
You're my gift,
My breath of fresh air,
My hero.
My shero.
My superhero who has sacrificed so much so I would have a fair
    chance at life,
You put your time aside to teach me to fight thru the challenges of life,
You taught me to be STRONG,
To right my wrongs.
You're the PERFECT SONG,
The brightest smile,
Who would do anything to protect her child,
Making me laugh when the world was so cruel,
Molding me with wise rules,
Kissing any bump or bruise so it would feel better,
And it ALWAYS did.
You would give and Give and GIVE so my dreams could LIVE,
You gave your all,
You give your all,
An angel who will NEVER fall,
Just soar and inspire,

DEAR FATHER

GOD's special work of art on display for me to admire.
You paved the way for my instinctive desires,
With an honest tongue, you would tell me the ways of the world.
There are no maps for the traps,

But you always say, "Just keep on trucking,"
Wise words from my favorite girl,
The perfect pearl,
My thornless rose.
Every day my love for you grows deeper,
I understand what you've done.
You've always made me feel important.
YES, I'm a proud son,
Who genuinely appreciates your dedication and resiliency,
I'm appreciative of the love and value you've instilled in me,
From day one it's been pure and true,
That's why every day is Mother's Day,
Because every day I can't help but celebrate You . . .
I LOVE YOU, MA!

MY DADDY'S RECORDS

The love for music naturally runs deep in my family, and it's always resonated for me: from creating it, to memorizing my favorite songs, to mulling over melodies and bass lines that swirl around in my mind.

No one put that floor-model stereo to work like my dad did. He was methodical. He took his time. With a cigarette dangling from his lips, he searched for music that matched his mood—the magic of the moment accompanied by the right tune. The smirk on his face made it evident when he got it right.

Seeing my dad flip thru and play his library of records imprinted music in my DNA like the grooves that were pressed into the vinyl he spun. He towered over me, but in the basement his shelves of records towered over him. This treasure trove of music, this mountain of melodies, was his symphony of peace.

They were black,
Thin, round, and vinyl,
But big enough to house names like Aretha, Marvin, and Lionel.
Some 33⅓, others 45,
No matter the size,
It would move you to hop in the ride and hit the countryside.
Nothing like a long trip,
A road trip,
After a long week,
'Cause hypnotic tones would speak,
Medicine would leak right out of the speakers,
Make you tap your gators or sneakers . . .
Gym shoes.
I'm talking about cats who been cool,
Who would use mics to melt their gifts on wax,
That later on cats would learn to scratch,
And folks would go to card parties to meet their match,
Their mate,
That they would later date,
Love they would make,
Pushed by passion, they would procreate,
Hooked on pleasure and the sound of love that would escape . . .
My Daddy's Records!

Sliding his finger over the title on the spine, he would select the record and then carefully pull it from its sleeve and remove it from the protection of the wax paper. Gradually he would examine it. Maybe he was checking it for damage? Maybe he was admiring it? Maybe he was rereading the artist label? He held the record in his dark-brown hands with a slow, loving caress, using his index finger and thumb to flip it from one side to the next.

Now Pops was a Mississippi boy, who was born down in West Point,
But later in life, he caught wind that the Midwest was the joint.
So his dreams landed him Up South in the Land of Lincoln,
But at first he didn't land the job that he was seeking,
Cause he yearned to be a DJ,
Jim Richards, aka Brother J,
Who had no other choice but to drive buses for the CTA.
But the story goes . . . that's where the DJ met PJ, who had Little J,
And the South Side is where they chose to stay,
And it was in that basement where me and my brothers would hear
    those records play . . .
They would just take my pops to another world.
When times stressed him, he had his Camels, malt liquor,
And the records became his girl,
And like a record pimp, he had thousands of them.
When I would sneak and take a peek, they would be surrounding
    him,
Talking about . . .
My Daddy's Records!

Satisfied with his selection, he would walk over to his stereo, pull
back the arm of the record player, place the record on the turntable,
and reposition the arm, allowing the needle to gradually fall into the
small valleys of the vinyl. The needle struck the rotation of his drug,
music erupted from the three-foot wooden speakers, and he sat back,
took a deep breath and a toke of his square. The sound was open and
pure, and the artists felt present in our home.

There were so many I would wonder,
How did he know what to play next?
Bumping Smokie with Little Stevie on deck.

It was astonishing,
Skills he was polishing up for his aircheck,
'Cause checks don't fall out of the air,
But for a moment he was captivated by melodies,
Hypnotized by harmonies,
Put at ease by sound that was born downtown on the Magnificent
   Mile,
And over in our sister city, Motown.
From Music Row and Broadway,
To Hollywood out in Big C-A,
He kept the gifts on replay.
From rhythm and blues,
To the blues and dusties,
To hip-hop, jazz, and the oldies,
The man was in love.
And it was that love that got him on the radio,
And it was his voice I would hear coming out of the stereo.
It was his named engraved on gold records,
Now it's my name engraved on platinum records,
So I guess one day, when I have a Little Jay,
He'll say,
"Check out My Daddy's Records . . ."

During these moments peace was guaranteed in our home. With
our ears and our hearts, we were all listening. With my eyes and my
spirit, love is what I was witnessing. Seeing this ritual, seeing how
much my dad loved his records, seeing the love he had for his music
further bridged my connection to a love that was so natural. Music has
always fueled me. Music has always charged my energy and soothed
my soul. Music has always rested easy in my heart.

THERE'S NO SUCH THING AS SUPERHEROES?

I was a kid who loved heroes. I love that they cared enough to risk their lives and look out for others. I loved their cool names, but more important, their superpowers:

They had X-ray vision.
They could outrun bullets.
They caught bullets with their teeth.
They could *fly*.
They could walk thru walls.
They lifted Mack trucks up above their heads.
They could transform, shape-shift.
They used street poles for bats.
They could disappear and then reappear in other rooms, other countries, other times.
They might shrink as small as ants or grow as large as giants.

They could hold their breath forever and live underwater.
When something was wrong, when someone was in trouble, they
    knew instantly.
And heroes always escaped the villains' clutches.

The biggest superpower of all was that they weren't encumbered
by ordinary human limitations. They were noble, doubtless, fearless.
And they always had cool outfits.

For me, my dad was the first and biggest superhero of them all.
Like the fictitious characters I admired, I thought he was void of feelings and flaws of his own—like them, he was immaculate. But over
time my maturity set in, and I learned that he was human—flesh and
bone. He was real. He did have feelings. He could feel pain and hurt.
He did have his own demons to fight and angels to protect. And he
couldn't always escape the challenges that he was faced with. He didn't
always win. He too was a victim of life's Kryptonite.

The older you get, the less you believe in magic and fantasies—
the Tooth Fairy, the Easter Bunny, Santa Claus, and your dad being
Superman. But when you're a child, you

Believe.

WHEN THE SMOKE CLEARS

The spring sun blazed thru the front room window, I settled in at the wood-grained dining room table with my #2 pencil in hand and my Trapper Keeper opened to a new page. Blankly I stared at my second-grade math homework as I multiplied my daydreams. My dad, who was home from work, quietly occupied his big chair in the living room, newspaper in hand. His boots off, his black socks rocked in the air. Off to the side sat an Old Style beer and an ashtray filled with more butts than a strip club.

With no regard for me and my young lungs, my father habitually struck a match, lit up another square, and blew out smoke circles. Like vultures, smoke clouds slowly began hovering over me, stalking my existence, waiting for the right moment to strike. The air became dry. My concentration had now completely deserted me. The smell was suffocating, like bleach mixed with ammonia. Silently I was choking, my eyes were watering, and the exhaust was clouding my mind.

The fumes polluted my math problems with more problems. Conflict wasn't my major, but my young mind became a dark storm: *What do I do? Should I say something? Man, Dad will kick my butt if I do!*

It was obvious that my father's peace pipe was warring with my peace. The same thing that relaxed him had me stressed out. Being too scared to say something, I was out. I abandoned my homework and dashed quietly to the bathroom, playing it off like I had to go really bad. With an empty bladder, I closed the door behind me, allowing this small room to transform into my oxygen chamber. Standing there, next to the toilet, I stuck my head out of the opened window, regurgitating the smoke that I had inhaled. The fresh air relieved me beyond belief. The outside air was my resuscitator. Life returned. I could breathe again.

Still having to finish my homework, and knowing my dad would come looking for me after a few minutes, I was forced to head back out to the dining room . . . momentarily. With my last dose of freshness wearing off, I shot back to the bathroom for another deep inhale. This dance continued. One, two, three, and four, sit, and choke, and run some more . . . breathe. Back and forth I would go, surprised that my dad didn't notice the merry-go-round that I was on, wishing that on my next return, his smoking habit would be gone.

FRACTURED DREAM

I remember our two-bedroom house and the fun times growing up on Eighty-Seventh Street and Winchester, those humid summer days chasing raccoons and garter snakes, having water balloon fights, and playing in the sprinkler. I remember how all the kids on the block would put our feet together in a circle, and we'd point at each in turn, singing, "Eenie, meenie, miney, mo, catch a tiger by its toe," to see who would be "it" first when we played hide-and-go-seek. Walkie-talkies were our first cell phones, and we used them to find each other when we played in the nearby Dan Ryan Woods. We caught lightning bugs when the sun began to set. Moms would buy us a deep-dish pizza from Giordano's on movie night. Grandma would take us fishing or to church in her great big Cadillac. In the winters we would build snowmen, sling snowballs, and go sledding down the two-hundred-foot-long hill at the woods. We had some good times. We struggled but persevered. We were happy. We never gave up. We did, in fact, take it one day at a time, and besides my memories of the cod liver oil I had to take when I was sick, the whoopin' I got when I was playing with fire and almost burned down the house, and the oatmeal baths I had to take when I had chicken pox, I really have some great, great recollections of those days.

Great but incomplete, as I would come to find out.

Our small household slowly grew from sweet to sour. My dad was busy pursuing his radio career and took a couple of trips out to New York City. After the first trip, my moms said my dad was excited about the experience and the good connections he had made. She told me he mentioned women and drugs being offered to him, but other than the standard elements of the industry, he successfully maneuvered around the distractions and had a productive trip.

But when he came home after the next trip, everything changed. All hell broke loose. My moms said she never knew what happened in New York that second time around, but whatever happened triggered a lot of pain and depression. I suspect now that my dad wasn't able to navigate the temptations so well that second trip, especially the drugs. I remember him resting on the basement couch, religiously smoking his squares, drinking his beer, watching television, and hardly coming up for air. He lost his radio job, and for the first time that I could remember, he wasn't working. He went from being one of the popular DJs, being on his way to the top, to not being able to provide for his family. He grew mean and cold, and a sense of fear crept into our home.

Skillets have wings,
Heavy black cast-iron pans that have learned to defy gravity,
Soaring like the crows outside my window.
This isn't the first time a bird got into the house.
Unlike that lost sparrow,

It knew the window was the only way out.
So it shattered it,
Free F$_E$
$\qquad$ L
$\qquad\qquad$ L,
Landed in a sea of green.
Danced with blades of grass,
Blades of glass.
Shaking off the grease that was left behind from the chicken being
$\qquad$ fried in it,
It woke the neighbors,
Startled the possums,
Then played the same game,
Lay . . .
Still.
Cloaked by the night air,
Hidden by the darkness,
Lost until the morning after,
Clutching the cold,
Searching for the warmth being lost,
Welcoming the night creatures
To lick it clean.
They too have families to feed,
Everything has needs.
So it sat there,
Rested for a spell,
Thinking, why has this sweet house grown so mean . . .

The fights began, the screaming rushed in, the wrestling bouts kicked off, more dishes began to fly. As time went on, the strain of their love volleyed their frustrations, but with no real advantage for either contender, the fighting matches continued to grow. Like a loyal, disappointed fan, I watched on as my team fell apart. As an eight-year-old kid, I felt helpless. I was torn between my fear and my ignorance. I couldn't understand what was so wrong. Why wouldn't they stop? Now, after going thru the challenges of relationships as an adult myself, I realize their love was being pressured by the changes we go thru as individuals. Then, my mind raced with confusion. I hated horror movies, 'cause they gave me nightmares. Now here I was living in one night after night, with midnight trips to my aunt's or grandparents' house becoming the norm:

8:00 AM: I'm off to school. My folks are already off to work.
3:30 PM: Back from school, back to the hurt.
5:00 PM: Scraping thru the cabinets for something to eat.
5:15 PM: Finished with dinner, but unlike the rich we were out of
    after-meal treats.

7:31 PM: The arguing begins and very seldom does it end.
7:47 PM: Dishes take flight, and under the dining room table I bend.

9:14 PM: I cry myself to sleep.
Chills run thru my body,
From my temples down to my feet.

11:55 PM: Moms wakes me and telling me to rise,
She tells me to hurry up and grab some things,
But I'm not surprised.

Midnight: I grab some pants, shirts, and my Buster Browns.
My heart pounds, as my brothers, Moms, and I quietly hit the back
    door.

Sneaking off into the night,
Yet again, we were thru shopping at this *depart-ment* store.

When the fight was in the living room, the dining room table became the fort my older brother Virgil and I hid under. Protecting ourselves from identified flying objects: the ashtray, the telephone, vases, and picture frames. Anything was fair game in this unfair affair. Whatever was in hand's reach might get tossed, so at times my folks tossed each other. As for my brother and me, we sat there ignored on the blue and tan throw rug under the table, peeking thru the open spaces in the wooden chair, big brother's arm around little brother, wishing we could run away from here.

"Stop fighting!" Silently my heart screamed...

Our home became a giant wrestling mat. Maybe it was their respect for one another, maybe it was 'cause my dad knew to only go so far with his South Side, do-or-die lady, but they didn't throw punches. Moms threw dishes and some slaps, and Dad threw around his weight and his voice, but I don't remember fists flying—unless my dad was punching the wall. Even still, the moments were jolting. I would hear a plate crash in the kitchen, and my little body would jump out of its skin. As startling as a crack of lightning, the sound of that breaking dish quaked my soul, skipped the beat of my heart, making me feel like the chaos would never end. It felt inescapable. If I were in my room, the television wouldn't turn up loud enough to drown them out. I couldn't make enough noise with my toys. I was imprisoned by the sound of anger and confusion.

I was stunned by the visions that were burned into my memory. To this day I can see my dad on top of my mother, holding her down on my bed, not hurting, but restraining her from getting up as he turned around and yelled at me to get out and close the door. "Go on, Jimmy!" And I went. It was my room, but it was their house, their ritual, their wicked waltz.

Tired of getting out of their path of fury, I wished I were big, so I could intervene and stop them. A door would slam. A window would break. The walls would shake from them running into them. My brother was mad, but I was scared. I was scared he was going to hurt her. Seeing how good my mother fought, I was scared she was going to hurt my father. They were young and full of energy, full of energy that was being pulled in the wrong directions.

Somewhere in the midst of the madness, my folks separated, but my father would still come around. One night, Moms told me later, she could instantly tell my dad wasn't himself. She suspected he was high on some kind of drugs, so when my dad hopped in the bed, my mother leapt out. She walked to the living room with him quickly following. Not able to escape the small confines of our home, he snatched her arm to pull her closer. Naturally, she pulled away, but when she did, they both fell, with my dad landing on top of her. There was a loud cry, and I ran to the living room to find my sweet mother lying on the floor with her hands gripped around her leg. Her face was grimacing from the pain she was in. Her cries were chilling. I hated seeing my mother in pain. I hated seeing tears stream down her face. Being a nurse, she knew not to put weight on her leg, and my dad, even though he was in shock by the accident, helped her up and took her to the hospital, where they learned that her ankle was broken.

A couple of weeks later, Moms would tell me, she overheard my dad talking to someone on the phone, telling him what happened to my mother's ankle. He said he came in late, got in the bed, and when he did, she jumped out of the bed, slipped, and broke her ankle. When he hung up, my mother said, "James, why are you lying to that man?

That ain't how it happened," and proceeded to remind him of what really took place on that unforgettable night.

When she finished, my dad said he honestly didn't remember much from that evening. When his truth was spoken, her intuition kicked into high gear, and she knew she needed to take some kind of action to counteract such unpredictability. Like any mother, she instantly feared for her safety and the safety of her boys. I can only imagine the stress she felt during these times.

The house grew more and more quiet. There weren't many conversations because everyone had a desire to be hidden and silent— everyone stuck to his or her own space. The television became the sole vocalizer in the house, as the mood for music was now lost. Our home felt stale. The warmth was squeezed out. We tiptoed on egg-shells, afraid to tripwire more madness. This was a home my moms found and helped build, but sadly she knew it was time to let it go. That had to be a tough reality to deal with. I'm sure not having the money to make a quick move made it even tougher, but living in a house with a man she loved but had grown afraid of had to be the toughest moment of them all. She was scared. I was afraid. We were all afraid, so my mother asked Dad to leave.

I do believe that my father wasn't an evil man with ill intentions, but if he couldn't be in enough control of himself to remember something so traumatic as breaking my mother's ankle, there was no telling what he was capable of doing and forgetting. We were controlled by that creeping fear. My mother changed the locks, and on the days when she was at work and we were home alone, her voice was stern with worry when she would tell us to lock the doors and not let him in if he came by. We did as she asked. My own fear understood hers, but my heart couldn't figure out how we had ended up here. How did we get to the point where I had to lock out my own father? I was locked in the house and in my thoughts, a prisoner of anxiety in my own home.

BROKEN UP, BREAKING IN

One day what my mother feared happened. My brothers and I were home while Moms was at work. Our dad suddenly banged on the front door, demanding that we let him in.

"I know y'all in there! I'ma get y'all!"

My heart dropped to my stomach and began to beat faster than the climax of a drum solo. Quietly my brothers and I sat like hostages—nervous and hoping that the locks would protect us. And then the banging and yelling ceased.

Is it over? Are we safe?

The door to the basement stairs swung open, banging into the wall. Like a burglar, my dad had climbed in thru a basement window. With rage dripping out of his pores, his eyes pierced down at me.

"Oh, so y'all wasn't go' let me in, huh?!"

I was scared for my life. I was paralyzed. I couldn't move. I couldn't speak. I sat there; he stood there, huffing and puffing, not looking like himself. My loving father stood there, transformed by something that wasn't him. The horrible stare-down continued until he finally walked thru the kitchen and headed for his and Moms' old bedroom. He emerged a few minutes later and left thru the front door. He didn't touch us. He didn't hit or whoop us. But his voice was brutal, and our seemingly secure haven no longer felt safe.

Whenever we were home alone after that, Moms called often. We weren't to tell dad if we were going to go somewhere other than school. She grew quiet. Her moods were heavy. All the fighting she had done with her husband, all the times she had ushered us kids out of the house in the middle of the night with our clothes in plastic shopping bags, all the fear she continued to feel was wearing down on her. She was solemn. She was frustrated. Her patience grew short. Unfortunately, but understandingly, she filed for divorce, internalized her pain, played Anita Baker's *Rapture* album every day to get by; she got a second job and a third, worked double and triple shifts, and like any great general, she quietly prepared for the future.

I was eleven, and I was deeply affected by their separation. My folks' divorce harpooned my heart. The finality felt fatal. Dumbed down by misery, with the aftershock of the fighting still rocking my world, I didn't feel cared about, so I stopped caring.

What's left for a child who's felt he's lost it all?
Unexpected falls go unbroken.
He crashes and burns.
The ashes are evidence of the guilt he wears.
His heart tears,
But no one thinks to look inside there . . .
There is where the anger brews,
Cloaked by confused thoughts,
A heap of human being without feeling,

Feeling alone is the worst feeling . . .

In school, everyone else seemed so social, but I locked my personality away in the prison of my pain. I was going thru the motions. At the same time, I fought anyone who stepped to me, disrespected me, double-dared me to push them back. Kids can be cruel and honest, immoral, and brutal. And I did my best at protecting the heart worn on my short sleeves.

During the earlier, happier years when my dad was around, I was outgoing and proud. After the fights and my dad left, I clammed up, feeling ashamed of who I was, ashamed of feeling abandoned, ashamed of wearing those damn Buster Browns.

I was beyond angry. I was pissed 'cause I had to teach myself how to tie a tie. I had to figure out how to talk to girls. I was left to fend off the wolves of the streets. And my sweet moms was left to carry the hurt for her children, knowing that we were coping with a lot of pain.

LITTLE BOY BLUES

You don't realize love is lost until you look for it and it's not there. A person's very first instincts are breathing and expressing love. When a child is born, and his or her eyes gaze onto the world for the very first time, you see the immediate love he or she feels for others. It's unconditional. There are no rules, no boxes, no limitations, or expectations. Hate doesn't exist here; there's just love in the purest form.

Children want to love, need to love, and they need that love to be boomeranged back to them. It's like most natural orders; it's reciprocal, the yin and yang of give and take, like oxygen and carbon dioxide, the ocean to its shore, our sun and moon, day and night, shadow and light, from hot and cold to young and old.

In this rhythm of love,
first we move our

left foot,

then our right,

as we dance in rhythm,

dance in rhythm,

dance in rhythm,

hungering for this food for of the soul, thirsting for nature's nourishing nutrients. No matter what city, country, or other side of the fence you may live on, love is natural, and when it's absent, well, there's nothing natural about that.

Why doesn't Daddy love me?
Why isn't he here to hug me?
Why isn't he here to hold my hand when I cross the street?
Give me a dollar so I can buy some sweets?
I can't see you, am I blind?
Why are you so hard to find?
I can't get these questions off of my mind.
I swear, I don't want that much of your time,
I just want to go to the park and play on the swings,
Watch a game and do fun things,
We can go outside and play a game of catch,
We can teach the dog how to play a game of fetch,
When it's hot we can go to the pool,
We can watch cartoons when I get home from school,
But when I do get home, you're never there,
You're never there,
Why doesn't Daddy love me?
I guess life just isn't fair . . .

BIRTHDAY WISHES

I have seen firsthand how pain's heaviness can fill the void created by love's absence. I will never forget the last phone call from my dad. It was my twelfth birthday. By this time, he and my moms were divorced, he lived in another part of the city, and holidays had been stripped of their magic.

Rushing thru his birthday wishes, he demanded that I stay out of the streets and out of trouble.

"Yes, sir," I replied.

The reason for his concern and sternness, he explained, was 'cause I had another older brother that he had recently heard bad news about. Even at that age, I could distinguish the nervousness in Dad's voice. This brother, he said, had been running with the wrong crowd. Lacking the energy to divulge all of the details, my father told me that his son, my unknonwn brother, had just been murdered, and he didn't want to see anything like that happen to me or my brothers.

Damn, I thought, *I had another brother?! He's dead? What did he look like? Did he look like me? What was his personality like? What was he into? Was he funny? Was he cool? Where did he live? Who was his mother? How did he die? Who killed him? What was his name?*

Being a child, I didn't think to ask these questions aloud. I didn't think to ask what his name was. I didn't think to ask what was he like. And being shook up, my dad didn't think to tell me. He was hurt beyond words. Due to the violence of Chicago, my father, this proud man, had to bury his young son. I now understand that this, at least in large part, explains his bouts with depression, bouts with guilt—I'm sure his thoughts often took him to this other son, who was apparently living a rough lifestyle, a lifestyle that eventually led to a fatal end.

We only talked for a few more awkward minutes. My dad wished me happy birthday again and told me he was going to take me to a Bulls game to celebrate. We never made it to that game.

Man, that call hurt. Yeah, we never made it to a game, which would have been a tremendous time for a kid who'd grown up in a city of living sports legends, but more important, I didn't get a chance to know my lost brother or hang out with my father.

For some time after that call, I would run to the phone whenever it rang, thinking it was going to be my dad on the other end. When it wasn't, I would re-feel those terrible emotions. I was like a sad hamster running on its endless wheel, feeling abandoned and lost all over again. I must not have been good enough. I was unworthy. Why else would he leave? Why else wouldn't he be there to love me . . . to love his family?

The questions haunted me 'cause he was there for my early days. He was present. His spirit was big. He was taller than buildings. He was an authority I respected. If he told me to do something, I did it. Hesitation led to anger, so I listened. His tone was stern. His voice was beyond commanding. It vibrated the floor, rattled the pictures on the wall—it shook your spirit. He was a force, a giant that I looked up to figuratively and literally. He was my first example of command. He was my father.

While writing this I had a chance to speak with a lot of family members who were close to my dad. After many phone calls, conversations, and questions, after a lifetime of wonder, I finally discovered my brother's name . . .

Demond.
Rest in Peace, Brother.

AM I MY BROTHER'S KEEPER?

With Dad being gone, the dynamic of the house changed. The responsibilities shifted. A lot fell on my older brother's plate. Like most older siblings, his heart kicked in, his instincts took over, and he became the extra support that my mother desperately needed. Virgil, a young teen at the time, was forced to look out for us more than he already was. He had to make sure my little brother, Sergio, and I were guarded and protected. He had to make sure we made it to and from school safe, that we were fed, doing our homework and our chores, and that we were in bed on time. He looked out for us even though he didn't have to, forfeiting a part of his own youth. He went to school, and then he went to work. He grew up fast. And because of that, a piece of his childhood was forever lost. For me, a new appreciation for him was found. We may have had different fathers—technically, we were half-brothers—but the love that we were taught and the love that he showed made our brotherhood whole.

VIRGIL,
Big Brother...
Dad was gone,
So you became STRONG.
Strength that was on reserve was now heard.
You were stern 'cause you were old enough to see what the streets
    could do...
Who knew?
The rumors were too true,
We could have been schooled on the way to school.
Some saw the next grave,
Before they saw the next grade,
Young bodies got laid out,
Love was played out,
But you showed it the best way you could.
BIG chief in a small hood,
A small chirp in the center of the woods.
We grew up near the woods,
Where you could hear folks SCREAM for their goods,
Their lives...
Some were taken,
Some raped and...
Some spirits were forever broken.
The lonely were unspoken for,
But the smell was LOUD,
Much louder than the dead cats.
Dead bats no longer circled.
You were better off wearing all black or purple,
You had a better chance blending in,
In the end,
It was just the beginning...

DEAR FATHER

You were a father with no kids,
Just little brothers,
Different fathers,
Same mother,
We fought over the same covers,
Toys,
Top bunks,
The last swig of Kool-Aid,
And what games we played . . .
Even still,
You prepared me for the creeps,
The streets,
The ills folks would speak when horns beeped,
When gunshots rang,
When the parks were stalked by Dr. Strange.
Frogs were found jumping in my arm when you took aim,
Character was built when Dad became James,
When love lost its fame,
We were drained,
Like when we had to clean out the gutters,
Our minds were often in it,
Because women took our minds off the pain . . .
Innocence diminished,
Little grown Rambos,
Our minds were our ammo,
And you were the Sergeant at Arms patrolling the field,
Trying your best to fix what we thought couldn't be healed.
Your will was tested,
You avoided the devil's deals.
You were an angel with a mean mug, but you didn't pass on us,
You wore your mask as a shield, but you didn't dash on us,

You taught us to think fast when you would blast on us,
Guiding us the best way you knew how.
It's amazing to see what someone can do with a little know-how,
How you did it I may never know how,
But I know now,
That love grows deeper than choice words,
The proof is evident that you're my brother's keeper,
Word.

YOUR WORDS HAVE POWER

My mother always preached to us:
The Golden Rule,
The Golden Rule,
The Golden Rule:
"Treat people the way you want to be treated."

I heard the Golden Rule so much growing up, but over the years I found the rule to be true—and similar to another: "What goes around, comes around." What you give is often returned to you, not always by the person you gave the energy to, but thru circumstance the special delivery you put out into the universe is eventually returned to sender. Your energy is matched. The yin finds its yang. The chickens come home to roost. You get what you pay for. You pay for what you give. What you speak may be spoken back. What you think becomes your facts, your reality. We do reap what we have sown. We cash in on what we have loaned. That's something I realized early on.

For part of my grade school years, I went to Foster Park public school. The two-building school had a park, a baseball field, and some of the neighborhood's roughest kids. Some were rough for no reason. The real tests didn't happen in the classroom; they happened in the hallways. They happened early, on the way to school. They happened in the playground after school. "Meet me by the monkey bars at 3:15" was the daily slogan. Fights were routine. A game of Off the Wall quickly turned into a wrestling match. The playground became a battleground, a war zone, and like everyone else, I was on the front line trying to survive the bullying, the name calling, and the esteem-crushing taglines.

Back then I couldn't understand the cruelty that some would unleash on others. Now I know better; they were perhaps dealing with life stuff just like I was. Some say home is where the heart is, but sometimes it's also where the hate is, as self-hate is passed to those who are physically first in line to receive it, those who wake up next to you, those living down the hall from you, those taking up all the time in the bathroom, those who look most like you . . . those you call family.

On the home front, when the war was beginning to rage between my folks, my own anger was fueled, triggering my explosions when kids at school would step to me the wrong way. After one of my fights, with tears in my eyes, I huffed and puffed as a rival classmate and I were broken up after a couple-minute bout.

"Why are you crying? You won."

I screamed, "'Cause I'm mad!"

And I was mad. I was steaming hot. Fuming. I was furious. I was upset with the conflict at home, and I was tired of the conflict at school.

One day in the third grade, my classmates and I were heading back to our building from the lunchroom, where we had been served up taco boats, sandwiches, nachos, old frozen vegetables, hamburgers, hot dogs, fries, and juice boxes. Full of non-nutrition and off-balance energy, I found myself being verbally attacked by one of my young female peers. Normally I was quiet, but the more her words bullied me, the more she fueled the other kids' laughter, the more I found myself being pushed past my breaking point. I blacked out! Quickly I went from quiet to striking, throwing jabs with words and cursing her out like a grown sailor.

Like a cobra's teeth, my words dug into her, injecting venom into her soul. The effect was instant. Damn, I made her cry. I didn't mean to hurt her. That wasn't my goal. But I did. Her tears snapped me back to reality, making me realize that I had crushed her. I felt terrible. Yeah, she swung first, but I went for the jugular. Not able to withstand my harsh rebuttal, she took off, disappearing like steam, leaving me standing there, feeling worse now than I had from the hurt she handed to me.

From the old to the young,
We hold life and death on our tongues.
Buried there within the warmth of our breath lies our outcome.
In come thoughts that are hung by our mainframes.
It seems that the same thangs we stitch on our inseams,
Is seen in the scenes our words paint.
We spit fire,
Blow off steam,
Become things that we ain't.
Our words either build, heal, or obliterate . . .

One of my favorite lines that I've ever written is: "Words are words, so maybe it's your actions that's doing the cursing." But our words do carry energy. At times we build each other up into unbreakable monuments. At times we hurl verbal spears at the hearts of others. We build or destroy with the feelings we verbalize. Our intentions are realized with each word spoken.

Indeed, our words have power, but like the ignored landmarks we drive by daily, we begin to take that power for granted. We forget it exists. We become blind to its effects. We may be reminded of how strong words are on Sunday, but we forget by Monday. We're reminded of the power of words when we hear our favorite songs, but we forget about their influence when we take the headphones off. We become lost in the ambiguity of our language. We lose the value of the words that roll off of our tongues even though those same words become the laws that we live by.

Our words lift us,
Break us,
Paint us,
Stain us . . .
Intention is written,
Spoken,
Our hearts are either healed or broken . . .

Each word and intention can be either a dart or a stepping-stone. We use our vocalizations to deflate a soul or bridge two hearts. Our rhythm is compromised or flowed together seamlessly. The energy we spew changes the course of time. There within the confines of our conversations our balance is predictated.

Syllables become complex tools when backed with intention. If my intention is profane, I can curse you out without using any profanity. The rise and fall of our tones stir the seas of our emotions. Strapped with the weight of words in these rough waters, you simply can't swim.

And we can't catch our thoughts once they're spoken. They travel, disappear, reappear in our memories like soft echoes. They become the blueprint of our ways. Stormy like the grayest skies, or soothing like the blueness in our waves. Either way, the words we rest on become our change. Fuel for our brains. Our spirits.

This childhood experience after lunch made me realize how powerful our words really are. In that moment I vowed never to hurt anyone with my voice or my words again. My mother's words finally made perfect sense. "Treat people how you want to be treated."

Often we lose to the contest of context.
Our minds are hypnotized,
Conned by text.
We breathe life into what they think we can't,
We are who we say we are.
If you say you're a star,
Chances are you probably are.
Our steps are laid out by our mantras,
Affirmations are claimed in conversation,
We steer down the lanes of our language,
Our bodies follow,
Strength is borrowed or lost depending on what we believe,
Opinions become the nucleus of our mind's dominions.
Words do have power.
Words do have power.
Words do have power.
The same way the world has cowards,
We're faced by fear.
Like sponges we embrace what we hear.
For some our blues become our blueprints,
Those who spent . . .

Those who spend all day thinking about other's thoughts,
Give those thoughts value.
They become our laws,
Our futures are dictated by what we dream,
We're beautified or bullied by what we believe,
What you spoke glues your hopes to your soul,
We feed on our inner visions becoming what we think.
Regurgitating the negativity,
The positivity,
We are what we speak . . .

I'M A HIP-HOP BABY

Like an addict, I was looking for somewhere to put my restless energy. Between the television and the video games my mind held those positions. I was itching for the fix they served. So . . . I watched show after show, played game after game, but the more I flipped thru the channels, the more I skipped thru the boards on my cartridges, looking for ways to escape the days and the hurtful hours during my folks' separation, I couldn't help but notice Virgil's music getting louder, and louder, and louder . . . and I liked it! Man, I loved it!

What was this sound? It was different but familiar. It was soulful but rhythmic. It told stories that my young black mind could relate to. It had feeling. It moved my spirit. It annoyed my mother, but was loved by my brother. So he played it loud. He bought tapes made by cool cats, with cool album covers, and cool names. He would take them to his room, tear off the plastic, put them in a boom box, and turn the volume up to 10. I was hypnotized by the sound. I was hooked to every word. Yeah, my father introduced me to soul music, blues, and jazz. Yes, my mother introduced me to Bob Marley. But it was Virgil who introduced me to hip-hop.

Hip-hop was the revolution of the young black story finally being heard outside the confines of our neighborhoods. These poets, these storytellers, these rhyme sayers, were brave and unapologetic. They captured the essence of how it was for us living in the impoverished parts of the city, but they did it in a way that we could sing along with, rap along with. This was the definition of innovation at its best. I was inspired. So inspired that I would find myself staring at the speaker, stopping, rewinding, and playing the tape again and again so I could write down lyrics that the MC rapped. With a pencil in hand I would write down their story, memorize it, and rap it back like it was my own. I was a hip-hop head, one who loved, resonated with, and appreciated this special and unique music.

In a time when the mainstream world thought hip-hop was a fad, these modern-day griots rhymed their stories, while the DJ scratched the break beat, while the break dancers broke and pop locked, while the graffiti writers used spray cans to paint the cities make over. From the pioneers to the trailblazers that would follow our way of life, our culture would be forever transformed. And I would be waiting for my big brother to leave the house, so I could dub his tapes.

Grandmaster Flash, Grandmaster Caz, Kurtis Blow, and the Sugar Hill Gang got us to the parties and made us dance. Even our folks were singing "Rapper's Delight": "I said, a hip hop the hippie the hippie, to the hip hip hop, and you don't stop." Yes, we were moving, grooving along with these hip-hop songs, and we were matching our style to the music. LL Cool J had us wearing Kangols. Run-DMC had us putting fat laces in our Adidas. When we weren't wearing Adidas, we wore suede Pumas while we break-danced on a flattened-out cardboard box with a boom box bumping Busy Bee, Three Times Dope,

Dana Dane, Big Daddy Kane, the Fat Boys, MC Lyte, Queen Lati-
fah, Boogie Down Productions ("One, two, three, the crew is called
BDP"), Kool G Rap, Ice T, Salt-n-Pepa, the Geto Boys, Public Enemy,
Kid 'n Play, Heavy D & the Boyz, Marley Marl, and the Beastie Boys.

Doug E Fresh was on in six minutes. With a cool English accent,
Slick Rick told us a "Children's Story." Too $hort rattled trunks when
he turned up the bass. 3rd Bass gave you "The Gas Face." Biz Markie
gave us the "Vapors." Kool Moe Dee shot off lines 'bout the "Wild
Wild West." From the music of the Furious Five, De La Soul, Roxanne
Shanté, the Real Roxanne, EPMD, N.W.A., DJ Jazzy Jeff & the Fresh
Prince, Eric B. & Rakim, Kid Capri, and A Tribe Called Quest, to the
hip-hop movies *Wild Style, Breakin', Krush Groove*, and *Beat Street* we
were living, taking part in this movement, changing how we dressed,
circling up in a cypher when the music was on, beatboxing, freestyl-
ing, kicking rhymes off the top of the dome, all while the speakers
got bigger and the music got louder! All the while we were becoming
more and more proud of who we were as a people. We had something
we could call our own. We had our music.

I was thirteen years old when I bought my first album, *No More
Mr. Nice Guy* by Gang Starr. I was already engulfed in hip-hop, but
there was something so powerful about purchasing my own music.
There was something so special about finding an album, a tape that
I had never heard. I remember riding my bike to the record shop in
Evergreen Park, a suburb bordering our South Side neighborhood.
I hopped off, looked around, not wanting my bike to get snatched,
and then headed in.

I wasted little time taking in the massiveness of the store, walking
directly to the rap section. Not looking for anything in particular but
wanting to buy something with the few bucks in my pocket, I started
at the A section and funneled thru the countless selections. With my
bike unlocked outside, I knew I didn't have much time.

Of the tapes my brother didn't already have, most didn't catch my attention—until I arrived in the G section and came across a white cover with two cats leaning back to form a giant X, with their arms crossed and their faces to the camera. Wearing black caps, black pants, and black boots, standing in a b-boy stance, they looked cool, they looked serious, they looked like they had a story to tell. The cover blared with big, red, bold letters: *GANG STARR*. Underneath the group's name in black, it read, *No More Mr. Nice Guy*. I thought, *What is this?!* The image, the name, the title resonated with my spirit. *Who spells star with two r's? They don't look soft but they don't look like gangstas.* I had to hear what sound would come from an image so powerful. This was the tape that I had to have.

And that was it! Without hesitation I ended my search and took my tape to the counter. I purchased it and was on my way. As soon as I got outside, I ripped off the packaging, popped the tape in my Walkman, put my headphones on, hopped on my blue BMX bike, and pressed play. In one push of a button, my life changed forever. The world, the streets, the houses, the scene all looked and felt different. From the very first beat, from the very first word spoken, I was moved by the music. The melodies, the voice of the MC made me sit up straight and pay attention. I was lost in the world they created with their sound. From the first song to the very last, I was inspired.

The best part was I found it on my own. I ventured out on a mission to find new music and discovered a treasure. I didn't know it at the time, but I had discovered one of the greatest hip-hop groups to ever touch a stage, a mic, and a turntable. Guru and DJ Premier, these legends in the making, did not disappoint, which is why I rode home in a brand-new world. Folks didn't know hip-hop would dominate the charts and become at times the number one music in the world, but those that shared moments like the one I experienced with Gang

Starr were already in love. Because of the magic pouring out of those mixtapes and speakers, we already knew.

I wish I could give you this feeling . . .
This hip-hop music,
This African rhythm,
These hood tales,
The hood tells our tale so well.
A break beat and a verse,
Studio recordings dispersed for the world to hear,
The world can hear us in our music . . .
Poets who began rapping to the beat,
The beat don't lie,
But it does make you move,
Dance,
It moves yo spirit,
You can hear it,
In these compositions composed from the heart.
From the parks to the bleachers,
Souls pour out of the speakers,
The DJ spins,
Scratches our itch,
Blends,
The heartache ends.
One jam goes off; another one begins . . .
It gives the streets hope,
It moves our mood,
Shifts our attitudes,
Influences and advises,
Never ceases to surprise us,
And make us nod our heads,

Bob yo head,
Thru this music we've moved ahead,
And found another way,
To play,
To pray . . .
These hymns are more than special,
They're gold for the soul,
Spirituals,
Lyrical,
The perfect soundtrack for the ground attack,
The grind,
The shine,
My love and inspiration,
Melodic meditations,
I'm spacing out when I use it,
My sweet, sweet music . . .
That was used to wrap poems around my mind,
It eased my mind,
Pleased me and mine,
Bringing comfort to hard times,
With hard lines that were scribed to soften the blow.
It picked me up when I felt so low,
It taught me to go with the flow,
This music helped my spirit grow . . .
Grow thru the growing pains,
Because of hip-hop the whole world has changed,
It will never be the same,
It will *NEVER, EVER STOP,*
I'm a Hip-Hop Baby 'cause I grew up on . . .
HIP-HOP!
Take me to the top . . .

PART II

PURPOSE

THE PRAYER

EPIC PRAYER SMILE TO

THE DAVE NOT EVIL DROP IT FEELS LIKE IM A TOP YOUR SKELETONS OUT OF MY CLOSET

DID YOU KNOW I WAS ON HBO BROKEN HOME NOTHING WORK ME SURE WAS IT ENOUGH TO RAI

WAS THERE A TV UP THERE FOR YOU TO CATCH THE SHOW BUT

ASK FOR THE TRUTH. TRUTHFULLY SPEAKING THE TRUTH HURT

IM BEYOND HURTIN, IM IN PAIN. WHY DOES IT HURT SO MUCH

EVERYDAY FIGHTING WITH MYSELF TO STAY REMAIN SANE, MY PEEPS THINK WE CHANGED.

MAYBE TRIPPIN OFF MY FAME, BUT IM STILL THE SAME. IM STILL

I KNOW ITS A DONT COME SHAME

JAMES. IM NOT AROUND AS MUCH CAUSE, BUT DONT CUT I DONT WANT THEM TO

TO SEE ME ACTIN STRANGE. BUT I DONT WANT THEM & FEEL MY RAIN N

FEEL ANY OFF THE RAIN BECAUSE ONE DROP, THIS FEELING WONT OF THESE THOUGHTS

THAT I CANT SEEM TO GET OFF MY BRAIN. NOW WHE

RAIN AND TOUCH YOUR LAND

I REALLY NEED TO REACH OUT FOR YOU. YOU'RE OUT OF

RANGE. ARE MY PRAYERS REACHIN YOU) IM STARVIN FOR YOUR LOVE A

IM BEGGING YOU WHEN I WAS LITTLE

PLEASE EASE THE CRAVE. I THOUGHT YOU LEFT ME CAUSE I WOULDN

BEHAVE. LATER ON I FOUND OUT IT WAS THE CAVE AS WELL

AS OTHER THINGS. AND WITH ALL THE SCARS IT WAS HARD BUT

I LEARN TO FORGIVE AND

I FORGAVE. FOR COMING FORGAVE YOU FOR MISSING MY BASKET

AND FOOTBALL GAMES, I FORGAVE YOU FOR COMING HOME DRUNK

BEATING ON MY MOTHER

AND HIGH GOING INSANE. I FORGAVE YOU FOR MISSING MY

ALL OF

TRACK MEETS. I FORGAVE YOU FOR NOT BEING THERE TO

GREET ALL THESE PRETTY YOUNG GIRLS I WANTED YOU TO

MEET, I FORGAVE YOU FOR MISSING MY BIRTHDAYS & GRADUATIONS.

I FORGAVE YOU FOR NOT BEING THERE WHEN I NEEDED ADVICE

DESPITE

FOR CERTAIN SITUATIONS, I FORGAVE YOU THE IRE

THE GRIEF ALL THE TEARS FOR ALL THE YEARS LOST WONDERI

IF I WAS LOVED. SOMETIMES ALL I NEEDED WAS A CALL AN A

HUG. I UNDERSTAND PEOPLE BREAK UP AND DONT MAKE UP AND SOME RELATIONS DONT

LAST FOREVER, BUT WHY WERENT WE TOGETHER. MA COULD GET A NEW

MAN. BUT WHERE WAS I GO FIND A MAN LOOKING BACK

SHOCKED BY CULTURE

It was November 1989, two in the morning, two days before Thanksgiving, and it was freezing. Virgil and I helped our grandfather load the last two boxes on the U-Haul truck parked in the alley. The cold air cut thru my bones.

Normally at this time, my moms would have already started the food for Turkey Day, but instead of preparing for coming together with the rest of the family, we were preparing to leave my childhood home of eleven years.

Once the boxes were secure, we locked the truck and headed back inside the house for one final walk-thru. I could hardly believe it. The home I grew up in, the nucleus of my memories, was now empty. And so was my heart. Everything I knew about life was connected to that house. Every good time and every bad time was experienced there between those walls, under that roof. My dreams, my nightmares, my bumps, my bruises, our family nights with a deep-dish pizza and a good movie, running the block, walking to and from school, the music, the lessons, the birthdays, the door that we marked with a pencil to keep record of my height, the laughs, the cries, the views, the outlooks, the friends, and the neighbors—all were tied to this sweet little home of ours.

Now, here we were, staring at the naked walls that once wore portraits of our existence, making sure nothing was left behind as we said good-bye to the house that protected us, kept us warm, kept us safe, and tried keeping us happy. After one last deep breath, Moms cut off all the lights, locked the back door behind us, and literally closed the doors to our past. This chapter . . . was over.

On the ride out to the South suburbs of Chicago, I sat sullen in the front seat of my grandfather's dark-blue Lincoln Town Car, gazing down at the ash of the salted roads flying by, occasionally looking up to count the highway streetlights.

I hadn't been to the burbs that many times, and when I had, I'd seen mostly white folks. What was it going to be like living there? How was I going to fit in? Would we get along? I was scared. I was nervous.

I couldn't believe Moms actually got us out of the city. Working two jobs, sometimes three, taking double shifts, cutting corners, clipping coupons out of the newspaper, saving and not splurging, she actually did it. Our great escape was becoming a reality.

When we finally pulled in to our new neighborhood, despite it being dark outside, it was obvious that we weren't in Kansas anymore. The tornado of life flew us off to Oz, the unknown, the land of mystique and wonder. Much like Dorothy in Oz, I was a stranger in a strange land, a fish out of water—or more like a cat in it, drowned and drenched by life's storms, frazzled, left to face the mysteries of the burbs, the unfamiliarity of a foreign world. The funny thing was, this actually felt more like Kansas than Eighty-Seventh and Winchester back on the South Side.

DEAR FATHER

City raised,
Suburb phase,
Left to fit my ways,
Sit my days,
In a place so unfamiliar.
The houses were so much bigger,
The yards were too,
Upstairs, downstairs,
Living room and a family room,
Three- and four-bedroom homes,
Our little bungalow in the city was only built with two.
I looked in the mirror and told myself,
"I only have you."
How would I survive?
How would I be received?
Would I fit in?
Get in fights?
In the city we fought,
I stayed up all night listening to the noises of thought.
In the city, the night noises were my lullaby,
They rocked and rolled me to sleep.
For weeks I struggled with the stillness of this new peace and quiet,
It was foreign,
Boring,
No gunshots or crossfire,
The caffeine of the city still had me wired.
But it was wide open for exploring,
My nerves sank in the pit of my stomach,
New kid in school,
New set of rules,
No approach,

Just hope for good days,
Just hope for good days . . .

The burbs' cloud of calm was uncomfortable for me at first. My ears struggled to adjust to the unfamiliar sounds that I would hear when the wind rattled the house. My rhythm was off, trying to adapt to this new dance. The blocks smelled different. The air was clearer, fresher. The water tasted better. The trees seemed taller. The streets were actually clean. The blocks were twice as long. The houses had more space in between them. Everyone's yard was manicured to perfection. Where was the litter?

The burbs were more innocent too. The tension didn't exist. Gangs didn't patrol the blocks. Folks only hung out on the corner when they were waiting for the bus. And the city's segregated ways hadn't completely leaked over to its outskirts. Quickly I found out that Lisa Bonet was right in her *Cosby Show* spinoff: it was a *Different World* than where I was coming from.

It wasn't all black like my past life, but it wasn't all white either. Clearly we weren't the only ones who had migrated here. This collage of culture painted a better picture for me of a multicultural world. The world wasn't just black and white, as I had thought it was. The carved out, black section of the city that I was used to wasn't an exact depiction of the colorful world we live in. Folks from all walks of life did in fact coexist.

I wished my moms wasn't so busy with work so she could have broken it all down for me. I wished my dad would have been there to explain the quirks of the society to me. But he wasn't anywhere to be found. Since that horrible phone call on my twelfth birthday, I hadn't heard from him or about him. I had to navigate on the solo trip thru the scenes of my movie . . . so I did. With the golden age of hip-hop as my soundtrack, I freestyled my script and improvised each new scenario that was being thrown at me.

First stop was the nerve-racking transfer to a new school. This wasn't my first time changing schools, but it was the first time transferring to a school with kids who didn't all look like me. Scared, on guard, waiting for a fight to come my way, I walked into that school prepared for the worst.

Immediately I felt out of place, but I knew I couldn't go anywhere. There was an ocean of unfamiliarity, and I was forced to sail on it, wade thru it. I had no island to run to and hide on. I felt like the black kid who had invaded an episode of *Saved by the Bell*. The school had its cool kids, its nerds, its athletes—all sorts of cliques—just like my other schools had; only difference was, some were black, some were white, some were Chinese, some were Puerto Rican, and some were Mexican. Within minutes of walking the hallways and getting the "new kid stare down," I was made aware of how different this was from my last schools.

That first day embodied all the elements you'd expect: not wanting to get lost but getting lost, picking up new books, meeting new teachers, and meeting all the new kids, at least those who were willing to speak to me. It was my first time I could remember talking to white kids at length. We were actually sitting next to each other, holding conversations, realizing that some of us were neighbors. We were answering the questions asked by our teacher. We were laughing together at the class clown. We were eating the same food together at lunch. We were learning together. We were studying one another. We were giving each other dap, shaking hands. We were breaking down the transparent barriers that society had historically placed between us. We were no longer on the outside looking in. We were in it, living it, experiencing the cross-pollination of views, crossing moats and divides, and becoming familiar with the bricks that built these castles.

What I was experiencing had to be a microcosm of what the pioneers of integration lived. Breaking down color lines. Sitting in a classroom that used to be all white. Unifying with cultures that you had barely spoken to before this time. Feeling nervous about doing something as simple as saying hello. Feeling tension from some who you knew didn't like you 'cause of the color of your skin.

I was forced to adjust to the norm of the world, a norm that my naïvety didn't allow me to realize. But it was a realization that I quickly enjoyed. I found joy in meeting new people and being cool with everybody. I finally understood what Dr. King meant by his *I Have a Dream* speech. I was happy to be involved with this process. I felt like a soldier for equality seeing clearly that culture was actually a prism of many different facets and many different faces that were from many different places and backgrounds. I got it, but my young mind was shocked by this discovery.

> In the city we dodged the bullets of the struggle,
> But it was the spectrum of the burbs that burst my black bubble.
> Civilization was grander than what I thought it was,
> Ignorant because of what my experience had taught me it was.
> My viewpoints lacked the dynamics of society,
> Its complex dimensions,
> The world's diverse position,
> Picture this collage,
> Art made up of different squads,
> Different teams,
> From the mocha to the cream,
> There are different people in different pews,
> Different hues,
> Different views,
> Can we all just get along?
> Find appreciation for the different songs we sing,
> Misunderstanding is grown when we're brought up alone,

DEAR FATHER

We isolate,
We hate what we don't understand,
Love what we're taught to love,
Put ourselves above the rest,
Our best will be realized,
When we realize that we all hold answers to the test,
Examples seen when our will is outstretched,
When our strength is diminished,
When our lives are on the line,
When help comes from those unlike our kind,
When helping hands are lent so we won't suffer,
When we see how it is when we're blind to color,
When we see with our hearts instead of our eyes,
That's when our ideologies are surprised,
When we deny our resistance,
It's when we'll learn that there are layers to our existence,
That's when we'll build bridges,
Stitch stitches for how we've been severed,
Q-Tip the Abstract said,
"Progression can't be made if we're separate forever,"
So I guess when we come together,
And the prejudices of the world miraculously stop,
The cultures of this sweet place will no longer be shocked . . .

THERE'S NO ARGUING

Ms. Argue was my junior-year English teacher. It was such a fitting name. She was smart, creative, and you weren't going to out argue someone named Ms. Argue. One day that's exactly what I wanted to do when my classmates and I arrived with our completed assignment to write an original poem. To our surprise she instructed that each of us would read it aloud in front of the entire class. *WHAT?!*

I was already sitting close to the back of Ms. Argue's classroom, and upon her announcement, I slumped lower in my chair, hiding behind my classmates, trying to dodge a request that I couldn't avoid. I stared at the words that I had scribbled on the page, embarrassed by the fact that I had to read what I had written. Why was she making us do this? I was good at writing notes to girls, but being put on the spot like this wasn't cool, and it was too late to play sick or get a hall pass to the bathroom.

The only thing that eased the tension of my embarrassment was the fact that this wasn't happening just to me; everyone had to read, no exceptions. One by one my classmates rushed thru their poems, and when it was my turn, I wasn't feeling it. I wasn't feeling the idea of writing a poem. And I definitely wasn't feeling the idea of reading it.

The day before I had struggled with what I was going to write about. Ms. Argue didn't give us any particular topic to concentrate on, so I didn't know where to start, or where I was going to land. Because I wanted to get it over with, I wrote about the first thing that came to mind, the cloud-filled sky outside of my bedroom window.

At first I felt silly writing about clouds, but at the time I didn't know that I'd be reciting my piece in front of the entire class. My assumption was that my teacher would be the only one reading it. I figured, why not? Besides, I was ready to move on to other things, so I sat down, gathered my thoughts, dove in, and wrote . . .

It Once Was a Cloud

As I sat in front of the window, I peered up into the sky,
Only to see a cloud shaped like a butterfly.
Its wings were large and round, like the rubber nose of a clown,
As they began to sway, rain began to come down.
The large wings allowed it to hover like a bee,
Its antennas stood out like the stems of a weeping willow tree.
As the wind began to blow,
The butterfly flowed gallantly, like water down a spring stream.
    It blew and blew, and down upon it the sun began to beam.
As the two combined together so high,
The cloud began to resemble a rainbow in the sky.
I watched the butterfly.
I watched until dusk was in the air.
Then I began to wonder, if I were the only one who cared . . .
As the sunlight no longer roamed,
I realized now that it was gone.

The beautiful cloud, the weeping willow,
The graceful butterfly,
The vivid rainbow,
Gone!!!
It Once Was a Cloud . . .

I knew somebody was going to clown me, 'cause I had to write about some stupid clouds. What was I thinking? Embarrassed, I took a deep breath and then zipped thru the piece. Moments later it was over. I was done and the next person was now wrestling with their nerves.

After class Ms. Argue surprisingly pulled me to the side. Without any delay, she gave me an A! *Wow!* It was the first A I had gotten in high school English. But before I could ride that wave of joy, she proceeded to tell me that I had a very nice speaking voice and asked me to perform in a show that she was putting together. Skeptical and shocked, I said yes, but overwhelmed by fear I ended up faking her out. I was a no-show.

Despite my childhood dreams of acting, my shy ways made me feel a little shaky about performing, but getting an A felt great. I was so hyped that I took my work of art home to show my moms. I knew she would love it. As soon as she saw the piece, her face lit up. She was soooo proud that she had me type it up and then took it to her job to put on her wall.

Over the week my mother told me how much all her coworkers, friends, and patients loved it and how they all commented on what a good writer I was. Being the encouraging mother that she is, trying to keep my newfound juices flowing, my moms asked me to write a piece for her work's monthly newsletter. At the time she was still the supervisor at the West Suburban Dialysis Center, so she handled little projects like that for the unit. Buzzing with energy and confidence, I went in to my room and started writing. Twenty minutes later I had finished another piece.

The True Meaning of Life

As I lie here in the slumber of my bed, my mind begins to drift.
It drifts to a mysterious place,
A place of thought,
A place of peace.
In the attendance of this place,
My mind begins to think and wonder about all things…
The most important being life.
What is the true meaning of life?
What is our purpose of existence?
What goals have our subconscious minds set for us to
    accomplish?
I found I was asking myself many questions.
Questions that must be answered to the best of my knowledge . . .
I pondered about this great mystery for hours,
I pondered until frustration began to dwell.
My frustration began to grow stronger and stronger,
Until I unlocked the door of my continuous curiosity,
My lack of understanding,
And my unanswered questions . . .
As I opened this door,
I was overwhelmed with a strong, wonderful feeling.
I can recall this feeling from my past, but it was never of this
    magnitude.
It was Love embraced behind the mighty door.
It was Love that gave people of yesterday and today the strength to
    carry on.
It was Love that restores hope in our hearts for peace and unity . . .
After a long restless night,
I finally realized that Love is the key to life.
I Finally Realized that Love Is the True Meaning of Life.

When I finished the piece, I walked across the hall to my moms' room and handed the piece to her. She read it and instantly lit up with excitement! She looked me in my eyes and said, "You truly have a gift." Wow! No one had ever said I had a *gift*. I wasn't sure anyone had ever told me that I was very good at anything. Her words jump-started my spirit and in that brief, but powerful, moment, I felt something shift inside. Here was my mother, my angel, my hero telling me that I had a *gift*. Right then and there, my outlook on life was forever transformed.

After putting my poem in her newsletter, I got the same positive feedback from her coworkers, my godmother, my grandparents, and other family members, but I honestly didn't know why people were amazed by what I wrote. I thought the pieces were aight, but by no means did I think they were exceptional.

I wasn't anyone special,
I was the nobody nobody ever noticed.
I wasn't good enough,
Light-skinned enough,
Strong enough,
Smart enough,
Good looking enough . . .
The other kids talked about my clothes,
The girls talked about my crooked nose.
Dudes talked about my shoes,
And when my dad didn't come back home,
My confidence was beyond abused.
I was washed up,
The low man on the totem pole,
I suppose they were all right,
So I became a boy with no ambitions,
No goals,

Just unreachable dreams that I dared not talk about anymore,
I mean, what for?
Why give the jokesters mo' ammo when they took the floor?
I already found myself believing their destructive descriptions,
I was lost,
Unaware of gaining on future positions,
So why would someone want to read what I had written?
Why would they want to pay attention to my words?
Why would they want to see how I was living?
Why would my thoughts be heard?
I wasn't anything special,
I was certain that I was just another kid,
I wasn't anything special,
And I didn't think that was going to change when I got big . . .
But it did!

A couple of weeks had gone by since I'd read my poem in front of the class. By now, Ms. Argue was a little heated about me backing out of her show. She pulled me aside again and told me that she and another teacher were putting together the annual Afro Club Show, my high school's Black History Month program, and since I faked her out the last time, I had to do this one.

What?!

Yes, I had dreamed of being on the big screen, but I was always too scared to get up in front of people. When I was younger, I loved the idea of acting so much that I would watch television and movies, emulating and critiquing the actors—when I didn't even know the meaning of the words that defined what I was doing! But one of the things that I learned from watching and playing sports was the importance of stepping up to a challenge. I couldn't punk out or back down to some lil ol' stage fright. I didn't want my fear to defeat me. I decided to do the show.

It was February of 1993. Ms. Argue had given me two monologues to practice, which is what I did every day after track practice. One of the pieces was about Malcolm X, and was so dynamic that it really drew me in. Already inspired and moved by Denzel Washington's performance in Spike Lee's movie *Malcolm X*, which had come out the year before, I practiced and practiced, hopped in front of the mirror, and practiced some more, locking in the words with the rise and falls of my voice, along with what I felt was the proper cadence, flow, and enunciation. I didn't want to emulate the style I saw in the movie, but I did want to match its power.

Members of the Afro Club and I were scheduled to perform late February on a Thursday and Saturday in our high school's Little Theater. But before our school premier, we were scheduled to go to another high school, in the Northwest suburbs, to perform for our peers. We took a long bus ride, and when we arrived we were escorted to a room big enough to hold seventy to a hundred people. We were set to perform for two groups of kids, and the first group was starting to file in. Damn, I was nervous!

The show started. Student after student performed and, so far, everyone was received very well. Me, well, I was still terrified!

Every time someone went up, it meant my turn was getting closer. My stomach would churn a little more, and a little harder. I sat there in my shirt and tie, running the piece over and over in my mind. I sat there unsure of the near future. I sat there locked into the seat of my emotional roller coaster, climbing higher and higher with each passing moment, feeling the depth of the cramps in my core, listening to my doubts screaming at me to get off before the big drop, but it was too late. It was my turn. "Put your hands together for James Richardson." Damn, here we go!

As the crowd politely clapped, I approached the microphone filled with fear. My biggest worry was forgetting the piece. With my knees uncontrollably shaking, I took a VERY deep breath and began.

I focused on speaking crisply and clearly, and as each line passed, that's exactly what I did. I said line after line, precisely hitting every enunciation, every pause, every word, and every syllable until I was done. I couldn't believe it. I didn't stutter or forget one word. Relieved beyond belief, I turned around, and with my head hanging down, eyes locked on my black shoes, I walked back to my seat.

When I sat down, a classmate very excitedly said, "Man, did you see that?!"

"See what?" I asked.

"You got a standing O!" he said.

"What, stop playing!" I said.

"Dawg, I'm for real! You didn't see those people stand up for you?!" he said.

"Naw," I said, and I didn't. I mean, somewhere beyond the clutter of my thoughts, I heard them clapping in the background, but when I walked off I didn't really pay much attention to the crowd. I sat there in disbelief, digesting the news being fed to me, feeling the confidence that was beginning to sprout in my spirit.

Shortly after, the first group filed out, and the second filed in. Like before, the show started soon after that. Like before, student after student performed. Like before, everyone was received very well. And in no time at all, my name was called, "James Richardson." As the new audience began to clap, I stood up out of my chair and walked to the center of the stage knowing this time I was going to do well. I glided to that microphone glowing with a sureness that I'd never remembered feeling before.

I was now aware of my cape. I could feel my power growing. I was no longer the timid, dorky, clumsy Clark Kent. I was strong, sure of myself, and the shy mask was gone. I couldn't wait to be heard. For the first time in my life, I felt in my element, and it just happened to be on a stage with close to a hundred people watching. There, on that stage, I felt at home. I felt at peace.

There I was, eyes wide and my hands waving thru the air, speaking crisp and clear, but with even more emotion than before. So much more that I tried to cut the air with each line. I wanted to peacefully and passionately pierce every present soul. I poured out my heart until I was done. And when I was done, I paused. I didn't rush off with my head down this time. No, I stood there and watched as the entire group of kids, fellow members of my generation, my peers, stood up, cheering and applauding. I couldn't believe it; my first time onstage, and I got a standing O! I wasn't sure then what I was feeling, but I know now that in a blink of an eye my purpose erupted, revealed itself, and I had fallen deeply in love. Not fully understanding the capacity of the transformation, I just stood there, absorbing an abundance of love and energy—exhilaration I had never known before. My life would never again be the same.

We headed back to my high school, where we continued with the performances. My mother came to the first one suited and booted, proudly cheering me on. There was no better feeling than knowing that she was in the crowd when I performed. After another standing ovation, I loved that she was able to see how the people responded. It further fueled my fire. It gave me something to reach for. At the same time, my disappointment was further fueled: just like it was at my eighth-grade graduation, when my dad didn't occupy the seat next to her. Even still, it really amazed me to see my moms' and other people's reactions to my performances. Teachers, parents, and classmates would approach me and tell me how talented I was. Parents would tell me that they loved that I gave their kids someone to look up to. After every show they would tell me I had a gift. And I mean after *every* show! So, of course I kept performing. It quickly became my fix, my release, my love. It quickly became my passion.

Because of Ms. Argue's beautiful, instinctive challenge, I was able to jump the hurdle of my fear. Defeating that fear raised the bar of my intensity for this newfound love. My sweet, sweet teacher helped me find my strength. Thank you Ms. Argue. I pray that every student has at least one teacher like you. Love you much!!

THE ROCK

I grew up a huge football fan, watching games with my dad on Sundays. That lifelong commitment led me to having dreams of one day making it to the NFL.

I wanted to play and experience those winning moments with the greats at their finest. I wanted to score the big touchdown in the big game with the final seconds ticking off of the clock. I wanted to raise up the Lombardi Trophy and scream, "I'm going to Disney World!" Besides Walter Payton, my favorite player was Jerry Rice, so when I did elevate from playing two-hand touch in the streets to high school football for Rich Central, I went out for the wide receiver position and nicknamed myself Jerry Rice's nickname, Gold Fingers. I was a baller, and I loved it. I was a part of a team, a band of brothers who fought, worked, learned, competed, joked, laughed, cried, won, lost, and grew up together. We battled on the field, but off the field a handful of those teammates, my guys, the fellas, the homies, my crew, filled the void when my dad wasn't there. We had different mothers, different fathers, but while we bumped Nas, Dr. Dre, and Snoop Dogg, while we played Monopoly and Madden and hit all the house parties, these cool dudes, these good men who always inspired me to win became more than friends. They became family. RC on three. 1, 2, 3!

One week midway thru the season as I was strolling the hallways between classes, a line popped in my head. I'm not sure why these words came to me when they did. Maybe I was inspired by the haters, the doubters, who cracked jokes whenever they got a chance, trying to convince me how inadequate I was. Or maybe my inspiration stemmed from the fact that the team was the underdog in the game that week. Whatever the inspiration was for thinking of this quote, we needed some motivation and focus. After writing it down and reading over it time and time again, I decided to pass the quote on to our head coach.

Not investing much into the moment, being a teenager who was still unaware of how moments connect to the next, I didn't have any expectations when I gave Coach the quote. My instinct said, *Do it,* so I did. I thought it would be something cool to share. I didn't know it then, but I've learned that when you find the courage to trust your instincts in those split-decision moments, you can create something exceptional.

A couple of days passed, and it was time for our Friday night game. As always, emotions were high in the locker room as we suited up, throwing on our pads, our sky-blue-and-red uniforms, wristbands, tape, gloves, and cleats. After we were geared up, Coach and the assistant coaches rallied us together, went over our assignments, and gave us a speech about focusing on the task at hand: winning the game and turning our bad season around. We were hyped! We all loved the game. That's why we were playing it. We had our dreams, we had each other, we had the moment, and we were excited to go out, hit the field with pride, and make the most of it.

Before running out onto the field, we lined up according to height, with the shortest being in the front. Standing at six-foot-two, I was one of the tallest on the team, so there I was toward the back of the line, my red helmet on, charged up and ready to hit the field. As we exited the locker room, the crowd was chanting and the band was already playing, sparking the crowd with school spirit the way the lights lit the green field. My heart began to beat faster. My adrenaline surged. It was almost game time!

Every team has its own rituals and routines. Whether it was after a long week of practice or it was time to hit the game field, the Olympian tradition was to tap the Rock, a massive stone outside our school that was about three feet tall, three feet wide, and painted in our school colors of red with that week's motivational message in blue. The Rock was our version of the Apollo's tree trunk that entertainers rub before performing on the big stage. It was our lucky charm.

As we marched the fifty yards toward the field that fateful game day, the team beelined for the Rock. One by one, my teammates tapped it and trotted off toward the field. After seeing the whole team carry on the tradition, I geared up to do the same. No longer blocked by the shoulder pads of my teammate in front of me, the Rock was finally in my sight, and to my complete surprise, it had my words painted on it in sky-blue letters . . .

THEY SAY WE CAN'T,
SO NOW WE MUST!

Shocked to see my quote on something outside of notebook paper, I trotted off toward the field feeling a new sense of pride. I was so moved by the moment—a moment shared with the entire team.

I honestly can't remember if we won or lost the game that night. Knowing that we didn't win too many games that year, it's quite possible we took an L (a loss). Regardless, I was inspired by what had happened. My moment with the Rock, this symbol of hope, has become a powerful memory. To this day I refer back to it in my doubting moments. It's a reminder to trust myself. It's a reminder that my ideas have value. It's a reminder to believe in my creativity. It's a reminder that I have the ability to inspire others when I am not afraid to share what inspires me. We all have this ability. We just have to exercise our beliefs and trust the moment. When we do, it is then that we catch a taste of freedom.

THEY SAY I CAN'T,
SO NOW I MUST!

IT WAS LOVE AT FIRST WRITE

In 1994, when I started college, I started to really look at the man in the mirror. High school cracked the door open to self-awareness, but it was within the confines of my college dorm room and the boundaries of Illinois State's campus that I began to discover myself. I didn't have my moms' daily commands guiding my actions. I didn't have my big brother picking on me, my little brother to look after, or my cousins to hang out with. I didn't have my crew's mannerisms to mimic, my coaches barking at me to make me a better athlete, or my teachers handing me scripts to learn and deliver. The "positive distractions" that I left behind at home left me in a state of constant self-reflection and self-realization.

Of course, college introduced me to many new people, and I had the coolest roommate ever, Syl, but the newness of it all made me feel like it was just me, myself, and I. This world was much bigger than the one I left behind, and for the first time I had to stand on my own two feet. I began to notice my character traits, my habits, how people responded to me, and the types of people I was drawn to. I explored my thoughts and found humor in my personality. My confidence and self-esteem grew. I was becoming more and more comfortable with the skin I was in. For the first time, without any interruptions, my feelings were introducing themselves to me.

Not only was my first semester in school filled with self-discovery but college itself was off the hook. I maneuvered thru the maze and made my moves. I had new homies to hoop with. I hit up all the parties. I was doing all right in my classes. And the ladies were lovin' me. I was having fun and being inspired. Biggie Smalls dropped *Ready to Die*. Common put out *Resurrection*. I had Tribe's *Midnight Marauders* in rotation. Outkast hit the scene with *Southernplayalisticadillacmuzik*. And the Roots released *Do You Want More?!!!??!* *The Isis Papers*, *The Autobiography of Malcolm X*, and *Soul on Ice* challenged my thoughts and expanded my mind. I was discovering a deeper sense of pride, a deeper appreciation for my culture. Exploring quickly became my favorite pastime.

The semester flew by. Classes like English, speech, and drama kept my attention, but I lacked focus in my psychology, algebra, and economics courses. I walked on to the track team, where I continued running hurdles, as I had on the high school team, but it wasn't as fulfilling as I thought it would be. I was yearning to get back on the stage. I desperately needed my fix. Despite the variety of college life, I was missing my first love, discovered in high school.

Around October I found myself going crazy over this girl we called V. On sight, she was beautiful, a five-foot-four, caramel-brown-skinned stunner. Most guys on the campus had their eyes on her. But more than her physical beauty, her warm spirit really reeled everyone in. She was smart, funny, super cool, and easy to talk to, and there was also something very peaceful about her. It was that peace that drew me in. Girlfriend had me shook. She knocked me off of my player square. Flustered, I was throwing my best game at her. She was feeling me, but she played a great game of hard to get. The more she resisted, the harder I was trying to get closer than close, closer than most.

After I had pursued her for weeks, one of my guys, who was trying to talk to one of V's friends, pointed out to me that Sweetest Day was coming up. Maybe you've heard of Sweetest Day, but if you haven't, it's a holiday that's pretty big in the Midwest. The easiest way to describe it is that it's like Valentine's Day in October, another day to honor your sweetheart, another day for guys to spend money. My guy suggested that we do something special for the girls, maybe we both take the time to write a poem. V inspired me, and I wanted to impress her. I wanted to get next to her. Immediately I thought, I can do that, so I wrote!

STRUCK BY LOVE

Over the short time that I have known you,
I have found myself wanting to bond with you.
You are a great person and an even better friend,
And I will be there for you to the end.
    Is it your beauty?
      Is it your personality?
      I do not know,
I just want you to be with me.
Why do I think these thoughts and say these things that I say?
Maybe it's because you warm my soul like the heat from a sun ray.
    I know we're going with the flow.
    I know we're taking it slow.
But I can't help but let you know how I feel,
Because what I think and what I say is real.
Where do we go from here?

I truly don't know.
Only time will tell, only time will show!!!

It was love at first write. I was really feeling the words, especially being that it was the first poem I had written since high school over a year ago. Beyond satisfied, I decided to type it up, and then I headed to the store to buy some chocolates and a rose to complete the Sweetest Day special. After getting everything together I headed over to V's dorm.

Nervous, I gave her the package hoping that she would like it. Immediately I could tell that she was genuinely moved by the gesture. She especially loved the poem and began showing it off to her girls over the next couple of days. I was the talk of the campus.

Moved by the positive feedback, I decided to share it with my English professor, Ms. Potts, and the rest of my class. Ms. Potts was young in comparison to the rest of my professors, but she was extremely intelligent and cool. When I first touched down in her class, we hit it off immediately, and over the short time knowing each other developed a big sister–little brother relationship. After she heard the piece, I received more of the same positive feedback.

Ms. Potts pulled me to the side after class and told me about this show she was organizing with her sorority sisters. She told me that she thought it would be a great idea for me to write a poem and perform it. Perform it! Yes! This would be my first time on stage since leaving high school, my first time on stage in college, but more important, this would be my first time being on stage performing a piece that I wrote. I had found my way back to the stage, and it just so happens that it went down the same way in college as it did it high school with Ms. Argue. Another black English teacher saw something in me and encouraged me to express those talents by challenging me with an opportunity.

I was ready to gear up for the show, which was called Retro Raggin'. Excited, I returned to my dorm room, sat down at my desk, fixed my mind around the times of the Harlem Renaissance, and wrote.

From Kunta to Alex,
From slave to superstar,
Our nation,
Our great nation has come so far.
We came to this land and our hands filled with cotton,
Now we're dancin' away on Broadway with our feet **NON-STOPPIN'.**
Everyone is joyous, because the war is finally over,
We now work for our infants, instead of our dogs named Rover.
What am I talking about?!
I'm talking about the baby boom!
All across the nation a child bears the mother's womb.
In the meantime we listen to the blues and jazz,
And we court the women with all the class.
In church we praise the Lord while sitting in the pews.
In concerts we honor the great Langston Hughes.
LISTEN to the beat, LISTEN to the horn blow,
But hey, we can't disregard the bass and the cello.
The dance, the music, the African soul,
In my heart, these things take a great toll.
The forties: By far this is the best generation,
And I'll say it again with no hesitation.
You can't stop this love,
YOU CAN'T BREAK THIS BOND!
Even though we have the Uncle Brothers,
Sam and Tom.
I love the forties and I always will,
But I'm thru playing my hand so now it's your deal . . .

Black woman,
Black man;
Walk proud,
STAND TALL!
For if we don't walk by faith,
WE DON'T WALK AT ALL!

I was proud of what I wrote, but there was nothing more satisfying than being on the stage again. The show went over well, and just like my times performing in high school, I was overwhelmed with a joy that I could only find in these moments. This show led to another, which led to another, which led to another. People were starting to hear my name around campus more and more and more. I was making a name for myself.

I quit track and started running with my poetry. The more shows came my way, the more poems I wrote. If there were no shows, I still wrote. Writing became intoxicating. Folks said they would find me in my room or somewhere around the campus in a poetic drunk lean or looking like I was zoned out in a marijuana daze. It became my drug, and I always needed a hit, another puff of the magic dragon. I didn't want to be off the wagon. *If there's a cure for this, I don't want it. I'll run from it.*

When I would sit down in the computer lab to type a paper for class, I would somehow find myself writing another poem. If I was at a party and the DJ played something that triggered my creativity, I would escape the dance floor and find a corner to write in. I used napkins, toilet paper, the backs of business cards, whatever I could find to jot down my thoughts. It didn't matter where I was at or what time of day it was. It could be ten in the evening or four or five in the morning. If it hit me, I hit it, writ it, spit it. If I had a new notebook, I had to fill it up. I needed to write. I needed to feed this love.

Toward the end of my first semester, I was writing away into the early AM. I could tell by Syl's snoring that my roommate was in a deep sleep. I could hear music playing in the distance, the telephone ring signaling a dormmate's booty call would sound off thru the walls, and the occasional group of voices would pass my door. But with a candle lit and my small lamp turned on, I'd created a soothing poetic ambiance perfect for the chicken scratch that I scribbled away in my notebook. The voice inside blocked out all the outside noise. All I could really hear were my words, and I made sure to catch every syllable. Between pieces I would catch my breath and think about my place, my space. The zone rested my spirit. I felt still in a world that never stopped moving. It was in these moments, these new moments of zoning out, that I would feel like myself. In this space the oddball no longer felt odd.

Finding myself in one of these zones that early morning, I strummed thru a stack of recent poems. Rereading "Struck by Love," I was on the outside looking in, observing what was happening to me, finding a new level of appreciation for my work. In that moment, I had a revelation, an epiphany about the new me I was experiencing. Chills shot thru my body. I was humbled but excited! So excited that I had to tell somebody.

With no remorse for disturbing his sleep, I woke up Syl. Startled and worried that something was wrong, he jumped up and said, "What's up? What is it?!"

"Dawg!" I said. "My poem 'Struck by Love' wasn't really about V. It was about me being struck by my newfound love for poetry! Every line, from 'Over the short time that I have known you, I have found myself wanting to bond with you,' to 'Where do we go from here? I truly don't know. Only time will tell, only time will show!!!' is about me and my poetry! Dawg, that's about me!"

Ha-ha, I can only imagine how I looked in that moment. There I was at three in the morning jumping up and down excitedly talking about poetry. Syl looked at me with the craziest expression and said in this very raspy, half-asleep voice, "Man, Jimmy, you woke me up for that!? You crazy!"

Not a second later, he rolled over and went back to sleep. And me, well, I was buzzing off of this high, speedballing from the adrenaline, moved by this awakening. It was the first time that I felt like I knew who I was, the first time that I staked my claim, the first time that I knew and spoke my reality. That night I became a Poet. And as I took my first steps into manhood, I would now be armed with one of the greatest gifts God has ever given us—The Word.

> I find freedom.
> Freedom finds me.
> I write what I feel.
> I write what I see.
> When you're lost in life,
> It's amazing to see what your writings will find.
> I write down the first thing that comes
> to my mind.

OFF BALANCE WAS
MY CHALLENGE

I would wake up in the middle of the night punching the walls,
And poetry was the one thing that would ease the
pain in my knuckles . . .

Times became turbulent my second year of college. Poetry became my everything, and with it, I discovered a lot about myself. Each piece was a blueprint of my strengths and weaknesses laid out before me for examination. My poetry gave my suffering and fears therapy, as my emotions would lie on the couch confessing their troubles. My pain became my quotes. My visions became my hope. My words were the mirror reflecting my inner reality.

The more I self-examined, the more alone I felt. I was shipwrecked on an uncharted desert isle, feeling foul and forgotten. I used the pen to search and sketch out the state of my soul. I now realized how pissed I was with my dad.

I never truly had dealt with my dad's abandonment or the craziness I witnessed when he was around. It wasn't until this new era of poetic expression and psychological exploration that I realized how much I had blocked the anger out. I had stuffed my scars deep into the closets of my sub-conscious. But these marks on my memories were beginning to surface. I was shocked to see what was floating in my muddy waters. I couldn't believe I wasn't as tough as I thought I was.

This revelation hit me like an avalanche. The hurt and the pain overwhelmed me, piling heavily on my chest.

I was so mad! Why did you leave?!
Was I not good enough?!
What did I do to deserve this?!
And what about Sergio?! He didn't get hardly any time with his father.

I just didn't get it. I didn't understand why I was left behind without a father around. *Why?!* Every question added flame to the fire inside.

This raw rage consumed me, transformed who I naturally was. Fortunately I found some solace within my writing. I would wake up in the middle of the night punching the walls, and poetry was the one thing that would ease the pain in my knuckles. My insanity felt uncontrollable, so I would write

and write

and write some more.

I would write until I fell back asleep at my desk on my pillow of poems. My creativity became my crutch for what had been broken and casted. Without the medicine of creativity, this pain would rebound whenever my mind would wander. I felt unworthy of anyone's love, and that made me hot. I wanted to hit something or somebody. I grew lonelier and lonelier. I grew angrier and angrier.

One morning I woke up and headed to my dorm floor's common bathroom. The halls were very quiet that day. Tired, I walked in drowsily like any other morning, not expecting anything out of the ordinary, but I froze in my tracks as I read the writing on the wall in big, bold, black letters, *NIGGA GO HOME!*

A surging spike raced thru my spirit. The words instantly engraved themselves on my mind. Who? Why? I was offended, tricked, and hated by my white dormmates. I thought they were my homies. I had no idea that they secretly despised me. I felt surrounded by enemies—stalked and vandalized by folks who lived amongst me. Shortly after, my feelings were pushed again when my moms called to tell me that my sweet, sweet grandmother had passed away.

"No, not Grandma!" She was the heartbeat of the family; she was the teacher, the nurturer, the matriarch, and the life force of our unit. It was so hard believing this news. This was the woman who had seven children and a host of grandchildren. This was the woman who would answer the phone, "God bless you," but if the unidentified caller didn't answer back, she would tell that person to go to hell, and hang up.

She was funny but tough, a firecracker but sweet like the butterscotch and wine candy she would give me. Most of all, she was a warrior. This was the woman who beat cancer. She was the woman who housed the brother of civil rights activist Medgar Evers when Charles was run out of Mississippi by racists. This was the woman who took my then eight-year-old mother to see Emmett Till's historic and horrific open casket.

At this point in my life, my grandmother was the closest person I had ever lost. The mass of weight on my mind wouldn't allow me to get a hold of myself. It felt like my world was crumbling around me.

And so my isolation continued. My grades continued to drop.

The force of the wind in my sails disappeared.

I sank deeper into misery and self-loathing.

Writer's Block

THE END.

THE ART OF FORGIVENESS

My return home to Chicago for my grandmother's funeral relit a flame within me to not accept defeat yet. I was alive—I had air in my lungs, blood in my veins, and a beating heart. Being back with my family in Chicago, I felt my pride kick in, reminding me that I was bred by some tough warriors who taught me to fight, who taught me to work hard: my mother, brothers, grandparents, aunts, uncles, and cousins. They were all inspiring warriors. My fellow Chicagoans were warriors too. So, in spite of my doubts, I decided to take a break from college. For the first time in a year and a half, I was back where I began with no direction or plan, but my instinct told me to stay. It felt like the right thing to do.

I leaned on my love for my family and city. I leaned on my pen. I leaned on my dreams. I was learning the lesson that when one door closes, another one opens. So, I took my mother's advice, adopted my middle name, which I once hated, as part of my pen name, my stage name, with hopes of finding the keys to becoming a great poet, a great man.

One day I was talking to my big cuz Julia over the phone. Julia is very spiritual, intuitive, and easy to talk to, and I was moved to open up and tell her my emotional troubles. I told her about the problems at college. I told her about the anger and misery I was dealing with when it came to my father.

Julia listened intently and then responded. Your internal storms, your questions, your hurt are drowning out your sensibility, she told me, but at the end of it all, they will make you stronger. She said that she understood why I felt so angry with my father. She told me that she understood why I felt the hate but bluntly told me that the only way to heal from my pain was to forgive. *With love dripping off of her words, she simply and sweetly told me that I had to learn how to forgive my father.*

Although I was suffocating in my anger, her words cut thru my chaos and seeped into my heart and soul. Her words made so much sense. I took a deep breath. I took heed of her words.

A couple of days later, I rode with my moms to her job to get out of the house for a change. I watched her work with patients lying in excruciating pain. How could my moms deal with the stress of this every day? The energy she gave was immeasurable. But like she always says, "You do what you got to do."

Out of the blue on the way back home in her Plymouth Voyager, as we took in the views of the South Side, my moms began talking about my father.

She asked me if I remembered the time she broke her ankle.

"Yeah," I said. Then I told her how I remembered it.

"Yes, that's how it happened, but that's not how he was telling it, because . . . he was high that night."

What?! My dad was doing drugs! I couldn't believe it. But . . .

The hard truth made me feel better. For the first time, I could stop blaming myself for him leaving. Knowing that my father was yet another victim to the drug plague, I stopped being mad at myself. I came into a new kind of understanding: my father was fighting his own demons. I couldn't blame him for that. I couldn't blame him for not knowing how to truly cope with his pain. I couldn't blame him for thinking this was his only way out. Finding this understanding, I felt that I could in fact start to forgive him.

I was asked to come perform at a church event on the South Side. Hungry for any performance opportunity, I agreed and started getting ready for the Thursday night performance. I remember feeling so alive when the show rolled around. It felt good to be back performing. This night I felt electric on stage.

Later on in the program, the organizers asked a friend of mine if he would sing a song. Without hesitation he agreed, but before singing, his voice grew somber and sorrowful, and he began to give an unexpected testimony. Tears cascaded down his face as he talked of his sister, who had passed a couple of years prior. Choked up by the pain, he took his time. The hurt was contagious. The whole congregation felt it and could understand if he couldn't continue. But he finally gathered himself and then sang the most beautiful song to her, as if the heavens cheered him on.

Watching one of my guys go thru this affected me so deeply that I started to cry. It was obvious that the hole in his soul, this void in his life, couldn't be filled by anyone but his sister, and she was gone. His void made me think about my pain, my void, my dad.

I began missing my dad like never before. I began to realize how much I had missed him all along. Not seeing or hearing from him for close to ten years, I truly didn't know if I would hit him or hug him if

I ever saw him again. Julia's advice of forgiveness echoed in my mind. With every ounce of my strength, I decided to let go of the past and forgive my dad. I did love him. I did miss him. And I desperately wanted to see him. I desperately wanted to tell him.

With tears streaming down my face, I lost feeling in my legs, fell to my knees and prayed as hard as I could. I humbly spoke to the Creator, saying:

GOD, PLEASE let me see my father!

I don't hate him!

I love him and I miss him with all of my heart!!

Please, let me see him so I can tell him, LORD.

PLEASE!!!

I begged and begged, and then I begged some more. I NEEDED to see my father. Unconscious to who was watching, I cried a river then collapsed to the floor to be baptized in my tears.

Witnessing the plunge of my painful free fall, one of my friends in the congregation helped lift me to my feet. As he held me up, he calmly repeated over and over again, "God has his hands on you right now. It's all right. God has his hands on you."

DAMN, DAMN, DAMN JAMES

I was so drained after my emotional release at the church event that for the next two weeks I kicked it, trying to keep my mind off of things, and I worked at my customer service job not too far from my mother's house, where I was still living. The job was far from something I loved, but for most of my shift I would write poetry, and it paid enough for me to take care of some bills, food, and gas. My routine was simple. I would go to work in the AM, hit the streets, hang out, chase girls, and try to drum up more shows in the PM. Most nights I didn't get in until two, three, four in the morning.

One Thursday morning, it was the same deal, in late the night before and up early for work, but this particular day, my body was starting to feel it. I was worn out, struggling and dragging around, as I got ready for work.

At the time, Moms was dating a guy, the first guy I knew my mother to date since my dad. His name just happened to be James. The irony.

On my way to work I bumped into him when I was trying to get out the door. Unfortunately he was there to pick my moms up to take her to breakfast. I wasn't mad my mother was dating. I wanted her to be happy. But him, I never liked the dude—he had an ill vibe.

"How are you doing?" he asked me. "What you been up to?"

"Working and doing shows," I said, not really wanting to talk to him, especially as he already knew what I was up to since my mom talked about her boys all the time. "You know, same ole, same ole."

My moms walked down the stairs. "Don't mind James. He's forgetful."

Yeah, whatever, I thought as they dipped out and I went to work, not giving it much more thought.

I sat in my cubicle feeling dizzy, feeling like I was getting sick. It got worse and worse with each passing moment, so I decided to go straight home after work and just connect with my homies over the phone.

While my moms was in the backyard gardening, I made plans for an upcoming show with one of my guys. The phone beeped, letting me know someone was calling on the other line. I clicked over and said hello.

"Hey, this is James," said the raspy voice from the other end of the phone. It sounded as if my mom's boyfriend was getting sick too.

"Hey, what's up?" I reluctantly responded.

"So, how are you doing? What you been up to?" he asked.

Didn't he just ask me this earlier?! I thought. He really is forgetful.

With all the sarcasm I could muster, I conjured my inner jerk and slowly said, "Working and doing shows. You know, *same ole, same ole.*" Not really minding my smartness, he said something else with this oddly . . . deep . . . raspy voice. Thrown off by his unfamiliar tone, I said, "Man, what's wrong with your voice? You sound funny."

"You sound funny!" he snapped.

"Who is this?!" I lashed back.

"This is your father," the voice on the other end of the phone responded.

I couldn't believe it!

It felt like that iconic moment when Darth Vader finally reveals to Luke that he's his father. Like Luke, I was shocked and disbelieving, looking for some place to jump and get away. There just wasn't anywhere to jump. Then it hit me: *Hadn't this been what I prayed for two weeks ago on that fateful, faith-filled Thursday evening? My God! My prayers had been answered.*

I asked my dad to hold on, clicked over to my boy on hold, and told him that I had to go 'cause my pops was on the other line. As I clicked back over, my heart raced like a ticking bomb. My emotions that had been pinned up for years were about to explode. But before I burst from the intensity of the moment, I blurted out: "Dad, I love you! I miss you so much! I miss you so much . . ."

As I spoke, my body numbed, and I slid off of the couch and onto the floor. The tears wouldn't stop. I was a broken mainline, a waterfall with arms and legs.

"Aww, man, don't do that," I heard him say, but my tears flowed more furiously. My dad's saddened voice couldn't levee the tsunami.

As if her intuition summoned her, my moms just happened to come in to the house. Seeing her baby balling on the floor, she straightened her light smile into an expression of concern. "Jimmy! Boy, who are you talking to?!" she screamed, rushing over to me.

I tried desperately to tell her, to tell her my dad was on the other end of the line, but I couldn't. I was literally choked up. I gestured for her to take the phone, falling to her knees she quickly snatched it from me, her defenses on high alert as she put the receiver to her ear. Like a five-year-old awakened by his worst nightmare, I sat there with my arms wrapped around her, holding on to her as if my life depended on it.

"Who is this?!" she demanded, puffing up like a mother bird protecting her nest. He didn't need introducing. As soon as she heard his voice, her own tears began to fall. "Aww, James, you just don't know how much you hurt these boys!" she cried.

After talking more with my father, my mother wiped her face and asked me if I was ready to talk. I told her yeah, gathered myself, and then took the phone back. As she left the room to give me privacy, I couldn't help but repeat to my dad that I loved and missed him very much. He told me that he loved my brothers and me too. Those simple words, which had escaped me for so long, meant the world to me! I was loved.

I WAS LOVED.

I listened intently, hanging on every syllable. With his regret deepening the moment, he said, "You know, I never stopped loving your mother." Hearing that hit me hard, as he began to reminisce, telling me how much fun they had when they were younger. I was so moved by his stories, imagining them young, running thru the streets of Chicago, and escaping the city whenever they got the chance. More important, I now knew that my dad really did love this queen I call Ma. I knew that I was created out of love.

His words, his voice felt so comforting to my soul—it was the same voice I listened to in the mornings on the radio when I was a kid. It was the same voice that echoed thru the rooms of my childhood memories. I listened to his voice as he apologized for not being there over the years. I could hear his sorrow, his regret, his guilt, his sincerity, and in that moment my heart accepted his apology.

LET ME REINTRODUCE MYSELF

I decided that I didn't want to waste any time, enough had already been wasted, so I told him that I wanted to see him. I got his info, rested up the next couple of days, got over my cold, and then headed to his house that Sunday. Nervous as hell, my thoughts ran wild as I drove to his home on Seventy-Second and Wolcott. When I pulled up, I felt nostalgic. The block he lived on was near our old neighborhood.

I took a deep breath. *What am I go' say?* It had been so long. I was a child the last time I saw him; now I was a young man. Thoughts fired rapidly as I walked up the stairs of his front porch and rang the bell. *Will he recognize me? Will I recognize him? What does he look like?* My stomach churned.

I took another deep breath as I paced back and forth. I heard footsteps coming downstairs. The lock clicked. I focused my attention on the turning knob. I took another deep breath. I looked up. The door opened. There he was . . .

I took in his features. When I was young, my dad stood as tall as a giant, but now I was the giant towering over him. He still looked cool, just older, much older, and like he'd lost the war he was fighting. Life had beaten him up. He was hurt . . . but *I was so happy to see him standing in front of me!!*

I swung back the screen door and lunged at his now frail frame, hugging him with all my might. I said, "I love you, Dad! I missed you!" He told me that he loved me too. He told me that I was looking good! I couldn't help but smile.

I followed him inside. We walked up the creaky stairs to his apartment. I remember thinking how small his place was. We sat down to talk and catch up. Here I was, finally telling my dad about myself and the family. Here he was, getting to know his son. I told him a little bit about my writing and the shows I'd been doing around the city. He seemed excited to hear the news. I was definitely excited to tell him.

Neither one of us was the best communicator that day, so we didn't dive into any deep conversations. We just enjoyed one another's company. My dad had the television on and turned to the Bears preseason game. The timing couldn't have been any more perfect. We watched the game just like we did when I was a shorty. The void I had been feeling for years had been filled. God really did answer my prayers. I thought, *Wow, I found my dad!*

We forgive, then forget to forgive again.
The voices speak,
Memories leak their pain,
We remember how it felt all over again,
We feel it all over again.
The past becomes right now,
Right now it hurts like hell,
It feels like a digging dagger dipped in death's spell.

DEAR FATHER

It hurts just like it did way back then,
The same story finds the same emotions,
Our past becomes our future,
We repeat our regrets,
We hang ourselves with our habits,
The cycle continues,
We sprint in place,
We run on oil,
We forget to let go,
We can't let go of our minds,
We reminisce,
Shed light on what happened,
We have flashbacks,
We flashback,
Quantum leap into yesterday,
Anger grows again,
Sadness grows again,
You're mad all over again,
Time spins,
We spend time,
Waste time on those emotions all over again,
Pretend like we don't feel it,
It feels fresh,
Our flesh feels the effects,
Our bodies grow heavy,
Hands unsteady,
The petty things carry weight,
We get mad at everything,
Everybody,
Nobody understands,
Nobody can,

Somebody will,
The stranger in the mirror still smiles,
The friend in the mirror steals smiles,
Give me that back . . .
I WANT MY JOY,
IT'S MINE,
IT BELONGS TO ME!
Happiness loves company,
Misery hates my company because I want to be happy,
I'm happy knowing that we have love for one another,
Love that's been smothered by life,
By wrongs and rights,
By guilt,
By feelings we can't shake,
The weight grows so heavy,
Anchoring us in the depths of our deepest ocean,
The potion is real,
The drugs don't heal,
They just numb our thoughts,
We wake and feel the crooks,
We stick out our stiff necks praying we won't be hurt again,
But it hurts again and again,
We forget to forgive again and again,
Before rebrewing the anger,
Our self-dangers,
Knowing that unconditional love is the only way to end this,
Unconditional love is the true art of our forgiveness . . .

LOVE LOST
AND FOUND, AGAIN

Reconnecting with my father that first time felt like I was living out a dream that I'd hoped for and didn't want to wake up from. I wanted to squeeze every lost moment into that visit, but I had no blueprint for making up for so much lost time.

At different points silence fell on our conversation, but what some may have considered an awkward silence didn't feel that way at all. Instead these gaps of quietness were like perfectly placed bridges over the river of anxiety that we were both trying to cross. What do you say to your father when you haven't spoken to him for over a decade? What does a father say to his son after being eaten away by the guilt his absence caused? Our words do matter, and outside of "I love you," what do you say?

Sitting together in his living room watching the Bears game was all that mattered—being at a loss for words was the right expression. There was no room for discouragement. I was grateful for the peacefulness and the reconnection of our spirits. I found pleasure in the small talk, the joy of reuniting.

To have remained frozen in that moment, hanging out with him for a few of hours was all I hoped for, but I had to get ready for a show at the club Rituals.

Looking back, I wish I would have invited him out with me, but the shock and surreal quality of the experience had clouded my thoughts. We hugged and said our good-byes, and I headed out. On the walk back to my car, I felt at peace. I was at ease. I was excited!

It was transformative. A weight had been lifted. A calm had been found. The link was no longer broken, and this gave me a new burst of energy. Knowing he was there, knowing he was reachable was a powerful realization. I felt so alive! I felt like I could start everything over fresh. I felt my mission was growing clearer. I had a better idea of what I had to do: to help change the world!

Everything was
in rhythm.
Everything was
going well.
Everything was
truly all good.

RITUALS

nspired, I hit the ground running and blazed thru the Chicago entertainment scene. A downtown jazz club, Rituals was a fifty-seat lounge that may have been small in size, but it was big in spirit. Rituals was electric; it was inspiring; but most of all, it was magical. Rituals became the hottest poetry spot in the city, one of the hottest in the world, and after a year and a half of being one of the house favorites, I was now the host.

My typical night opener went something like this:

"Can I get a clap check?!

I said, CAN I GET A CLAP CHECK?!
I can't hear those fingers snapping,
I need y'all to put your hands together,
Stomp your feet,
Make some noise,

Let's get some energy up in here!
Yeah, that feels good!"

Every Sunday night the line into the building wrapped around the corner. Hundreds squeezed in, packing the room from wall to wall, anticipating a new awakening. Candlelight danced on the tables and the faces and bodies of the audience. While libations filled the glasses, the incense of Nag Champa and anticipation filled the air. Mark Stampley and his band, Eclipse of the Moon, were tuning up in the background, ready to back us poets up.

"Y'all give it up for Mark Stampley and Eclipse of the Moon.
They play so beautifully,
Don't you agree?!
Don't you agree?!

We have the most amazing poets, wordsmiths, singers, and MCs in
    the land . . .
In the world.
And they're here to lift you up,
And touch you in a way you've never been touched,
When I tell y'all, you're in for a treat,
YOU'RE IN FOR A TREAT!
Are y'all ready for a good night?
Say, yeah!"

"YEAH!!"

I get so worked up on stage. You know how you feel when you go to church and catch the Spirit? You know how filled up you feel? Well, that's how I feel whenever I get on stage; I get filled up so much that

I want to share that sensation with the crowd. In an attempt to share that feeling at Rituals, I would start a call and response with my audience. I would pose the ceremonial command, and we would proceed to breathe each other's energy in and out, out and in:

"Whenever you hear me say,
'And the church says . . .'
I want you to say, 'AIGHT!'

And the church says . . ."

"AIGHT!!"

"And the church says . . ."

"AIGHT!!"

"All right, our first poet to the microphone is . . .
Well, before we get started, do y'all mind if I warm it up a lil bit?"

"Yeah!"

"Y'all mind if I do a lil something, something?"

"Do that, Poet!"

"Let's go, J. Ivy!"

"Aight, let's see, what are y'all in the mood for?"

"Do 'Transformation'!"

"Do 'Moon Cry'!"

"Do 'Wings'!"

"Man, y'all got requests tonight!
That's cool! That's cool . . .
Mark, let's do 'Wings' . . ."

Whether you were a poet or a witness, you knew that your spirit would be lifted by the words and the stories told between these walls. Backed by Mark Stampley's band, each poet would let his or her creativity open the door to your spirit and introduce you to new heights. Each poet had a way of transforming you and your thoughts. Each poet had a special way of enlightening you. We magically knew what was on your mind. We were poetic psychics. We were your sub-conscious being projected in front of you onto a stage. Whether the piece was theatrical, lyrical, or straight to the point, whether the piece was memorized or read off of the paper being held, each syllable spoken, each phrase that was delivered taught you something new about yourself. This place housed an explosion of epiphanies. Poetically speaking, it truly was a ritual.

"And the church says . . ."

"AIGHT!"

"And the church says . . ."

"AIGHT!!"

"Well, that's it for the first half.

Did y'all enjoy yourselves?!
I'm glad to hear it,
Glad to know it,
Now, I want you to know that we have an amazing line up for the
    second half,
But right now we're going take a little break,
And tune in to the sounds of DJ INC,
So, stretch out, get a drink, get your dance on, and tip your bartender,
And like I tell y'all every week,
Y'all go ahead and mingle if you're single,
But if you ain't,
You can't!
We ain't trying to get nobody in trouble . . .
INC, let's go!"

Leading the way as the host, as the captain of this ship, I cherished
the duty of maintaining the flow as well as bringing it when it was
time to fill the gaps. Every other poet in the house was bringing it,
so I had no other choice but to be on my A game. I had to bring
it. I wanted to bring it. I didn't want to be the one to blow this high.

So, week to week, I spilled my soul at Rituals. I dove off of my poetic
plank, swam in the excellence of this ecstasy, gladly sank into the deep
end, and fell in love with the sport. The competition wasn't official,
but you always were inspired to be on point. These Chicago poets
motivated each other to become better by showing off our unique
styles, words, and deliveries. That challenge of proving yourself over
and over again sharpened your tools, tools that you loved to nurture.
It pushed you to be a beast with the beauty you spoke.

Besides from the other poets, motivation and inspiration were
drawn from the crowd itself. Chicago has the hardest crowds I have
ever performed for. This is a blue-collar town of people who yearn to

be entertained when they get off of their jobs. Life is stressful in the Chi. Winters are cold. The summer humidity is sticky. The jobs don't pay enough. The streets take our children and don't give them back. Dreams get snatched away. And drama is the spice on top of it all. So when folks take their precious time to come out and spend their hard-earned money to come check out the show, you better not disappoint.

"Thank you for coming out . . .
You could have been anywhere else in the world,
But it's so good to see you're here with us tonight."

If you're wack, don't be surprised when they let you know. But if they love you, man, if they love you, they'll love you forever. There's no feeling like gaining that Chicago love.

"And the church says . . ."

"AIGHT!!"

As your skills were fine-tuned, you moved without knowing why you were moving. You touched people without knowing you were touching them. It was thrilling for me, so I would hop on stage and have fun, not necessarily considering the effect I was having on others. You just did what you loved to do.

I JUST GOT MY WINGS

Cause of the attention I was receiving at Rituals and around town, I was often invited to perform at other events. Being young, I was still grasping the true power of the word, but I was always excited to go out and exercise my passion.

One day my church asked some of the youth ministries to lift the spirits at a West Side shelter for recovering alcoholics and drug addicts.

This was tough for me, 'cause I was used to standing in a room filled with happy faces and bright smiles. Here I was in a setting where everyone's heart and spirit had been broken. The energy was low. The room was cold. I didn't know what kind of reaction to expect. I didn't know the depth of what this crowded room had been thru, but I could feel that it was more than any of us could handle.

Lost as to what piece I might perform, I couldn't answer the question running around my brain: *How was I going to be able to help them?* The MC came out and announced my turn: "Coming to the stage, please put your hands together for J. Ivy."

Time was up. I had to decide. My spirit spoke to me, my instinct raised its hand, and in a split second I decided to perform "Wings," praying that my words would lift their spirits.

Hello!
Is there anybody out there?
I got a story to tell,
Somebody's got to hear my story,
Is there anybody out there listening to my story?
My Story,
My Story.

As always, I immersed myself into the piece. The Spirit had now taken over. The nervousness caused by the lonely eyes looking back at me no longer mattered. I found my calm. Like a jazz musician's, my notes, my voice began to rise and fall in between the beat of the poem. I let go and dove into the true essence of the words. I lived in it. I became it and brought it to life there on the stage. With my audience's attentive ears and eyes on me, I maneuvered thru the mazes of phrases. I spoke not only with my words but with my body, my face, my hands.

Today, I planned on going to see my girly,
'Cause Mr. Furley and his three peeps ain't keeping good company.
Luckily, I got enough change to fill my tank up to a quarter,
So I guess I ought to roll out, like coins out holey pockets.
Man, it's hot as hell, like rockets on launch pads,
But like my dad,
I'm taking off with the wind beneath my wings.

My wings . . .
Ooh, them Harold's Chicken wings are starting to smell so good.
On the norm I would stop,
But see I'ma keep going like flowing rivers and streams.
I see this green light evaporate as the red halts my actions like a dam.
But I'm not trippin',
Cause I'm receiving mental satisfaction from this ma'am on the
    corner.
"What's up, girl..."
But as I look upon her, she begins to shiver, then scream.
Simultaneously,
I could feel the warmth of a bright gleam of light
Break thru the door to my left.
I take a deep breath as me and another being
Exchange words . . .

[With my right hand forming the shape of a gun, I stretched out my arm
and pointed it at an imaginary car.]

CLICK. CLICK.
  "Get out the car!"
HUH?!
  "GET OUT THE CAR!!"

[Looking back and forth, I moved back and forth between playing myself
and playing this character named Angel, my face transformed from a feared
driver to an enraged carjacker.]

Angel?
Angel?
Is that you?!

It's me, Jay,
Girl, why you trippin'? Put down the gun!!

[With my hands released from the fictitious steering wheel, I lifted them both in
the air in the direction of where Angel would be towering over me as I begged for
her merciful understanding.]

"Look, I don't care who you are!
Get out the car!"
Angel, man, you was my shorty when we were shorties.
You was the first girl I kissed.
"Get out the ride now!"
Angel!
"Now!"
ANGEL!
"NOW!!"
ANGEL!!!

POW...POW...POW.

[To the floor my body slowly collapsed. I paused and then rose to my feet
as if my spirit were now telling the story.]

I guess my actions were too slow,
Because I watched as her right index glided thru the air,
Pulling back on the crescent-moon-shaped trigger.
Releasing a horrific sound,
More horrific than that word n*gga,
"NIGGA, COME ON!"
Some cat said moments after my skull was pierced by those metallic
    demons.

DEAR FATHER

I was screaming loud,
But really wasn't saying nothing,
Cause my heart was pumping silently,
And everybody had their eye on me like those spies for World War III.
But me,
Well see,
My eye was on the sparrow sitting on top of the red light,
As my soul began to take flight onto another level,
I started thinking about that devil that's been trying to dig me under
    like shovels.
So I'm pulling thru like pulleys so I can reside on 7 North Heavenly
    Lane,
'Cause that bright light from above was beginning to rain onto me,
Like thunderstorms,

[As the poem moved, so did my body. So did my emotions. I moved with the waves
of the piece, leaving the valley of it and rising to the crescendos of its peaks...]

My spiritual tears began their pouring as I continued soaring toward
    the Light.
The Light . . .
I could feel my soul absorb the Light as I continued my flight upward,
Like rubber handles on escalators,
Or Outkast on them "Elevators,"
So I guess I'll see you gators later,
Because this kid here . . . has—just—got—his—wings!

[After the storm of it all, the light began to shine again. Within the poem
    I found the smile that was smothered by the pain of the character.
    I found his joy. I discovered the life that this calamity tried to kill.
        I stretched out my arms... my wings.]

I don't believe it,
I actually got my wings!
Somebody tell my moms that her baby boy is all right,
'Cause I just got my wings!
Somebody tell my brothers that I love 'em,
But I just got my wings!
Somebody tell my boys that I ain't go be there to kick it no mo',
'Cause I just got my wings!
Somebody tell my girly that I ain't go make it over today,
'Cause I just got my wings!
Somebody tell Angel,
My sweet,
Sweet,
Sweet,
Sweet,
angel of death,
That I'm all right,
'Cause I just got my wings . . .
Everything is looking up like 7,
'Cause I'm feeling heavenly with . . .
My wings.
My wings!
Hello,
Is there anybody out there listening to my story?!
Anybody,
Somebody,
Please tell everybody,
That I'm alright,
'Cause I Just Got My Wings!
I Just Got My Wings!
I Just Got My Wings!
I Just Got My Wings!

After the performance, folks complimented me on the poem and thanked me for coming to see them. Relieved that the piece wasn't off base for the occasion, I graciously thanked them for the love.

It was just about time for us to head out when I was approached by a woman in her mid-thirties. Although her face was heavy with the bags her eyes carried, although the gravity of her sadness pulled her demeanor close to the ground, although her mood had been sunken like a broken ship, her spirit instantly caught my attention.

Before I could say anything, she began to speak, telling me a story like none I had ever heard. She explained that she was recovering from a series of life-shattering experiences that had almost broken her spirit beyond repair: her father had passed away in January; her husband had passed away in February; and her son had passed away in March. I couldn't imagine losing three people so close to my heart and so close in time. I wouldn't wish that on my worst enemy. How was she still standing? I understood why her life had turned to addiction. She was desperately trying to escape.

She took a deep breath, and her energy lifted slightly. She said hearing "Wings" had brought her the first peace since the passing of her family. I was stuck. What could I say to that? "Thank you" didn't seem like enough, but it was all I had to offer. *My words helped her find peace?!*

The thought replayed over and over again as we hugged and then departed from one another: *My words helped her find peace?! What?!* This was a poem I thought of while sitting in my car, staring at the glare of a red light. My idea was simply to write a story about something that could happen in that moment. A carjacking seemed plausible enough to write about, so I wrote it. After writing it, I had joy performing it. Maybe I had been naïve up to that point, but I just didn't realize its possible effect. Because of that woman's story, the meaning and purpose of my work grew tremendously. I realized that my gift of living and breathing hope thru poetry was powerful, precious, and at that moment, I knew if it could help her, someone who was forced to bear so much, I could help others too.

"And the church says . . ."

"AMEN!!"

THE TEXTURE OF SOUL

One cold, snowy Sunday, I headed down to Rituals with Tarrey, this incredibly beautiful, sexy, young lady I was now dating. We were both anticipating another amazing night. The cold was ridiculous that night, so after we parked, we planned to make a mad dash like two track stars for the door.

We stepped out to cut thru the arctic chill, but this homeless cat suddenly and humbly waved us down, stopping us in our tracks. He asked us if he could clean our windows for some change. Like most major cities, Chicago is flooded with the less fortunate. Sadly, after getting stopped a thousand times, you grow immune to them, you become accustomed to them. So much so that you start passing them up, shaking off any remorse you may have felt.

The bitter cold motivated us to keep it moving, but we sensed something different about this scrappy, fiftysomething-year-old man. We could tell he hadn't showered in a while. His shoes were broken in and broken out. His coat was holed by time and maybe the streets he slept on. His hat and old gloves were ventilated too from the wear and tear. I couldn't help but think, *I just got out of a heated car, and I'm shivering. How is he living in this deep freezer?*

How was he spending hours out in this brutal cold that I had no intention of standing in for more than a minute or two? I was puzzled by his strength. Even more confusing was the joy that he expressed. Despite the cause and effects that brought him to this point, despite the conditions he was dwelling in, he was beyond pleasant. He was jolly. Resting behind his clouds of breath lay the biggest, brightest smile that I had seen on a stranger in a while. He may have been down and out, but his will to live was burning bright. That willingness, that appreciation for life, was translated into the kindheartedness he expressed. With that infectious smile plastered on his face, he instantly became one of the nicest people I'd ever met.

Naturally, we agreed to accept his help. We couldn't say no. We didn't want to say no. We would happily bear the cold a little bit longer if it meant helping someone this nice. His smile was ongoing as he began to clean the windows. While he worked he told us he had plans of using the money to get a haircut for an upcoming job interview. Knowing we were helping him reach a goal made the moment that more special.

Most times when you do help folks on the streets, you're not sure where the money is going. I've had homeless people ask me for money for food, and moments later I'd see them walking into the liquor store. There have been times when I've given food instead of money, and I've seen that food end up on the ground. But this man was different. With every bit of my spirit, I knew he was telling the truth. As he finished cleaning the windows, I knew he was going to use the money to try and better his situation. We naturally wanted to remember this pleasant being, so we asked him for his name. With that golden smile still on his face, he chuckled with joy and said, "Raymond."

Raymond's bashful cheer reminded me of how I felt when I was five, waking up on Christmas Day with a host of gifts flanking the tree. His joy was innocent and pleasant. It was sweet and kind. It was contagious. It was touching watching him as he stepped from side to side, ecstatic with the few bucks we gave him.

Excited to return the love, he said he wanted to sing a song for us. "A song?" we replied. "Of course!" Without further hesitation, Raymond jumped into his vocal escapade.

Being in the arts, I'd heard thousands of singers and poets. It's beautiful to see people express themselves, but some are just extra special. Some have a way of tapping your core, moving you in a way you've never been moved. In all my years, I've still never been moved quite like Raymond moved me on that cold winter night.

This down-and-out man, blanketed by a smile, closed his eyes, opened the depths of his soul, and began singing Earth, Wind & Fire's "Reasons." It was as if a piece of heaven poured out of him. His voice climbed into falsetto moments and fell into low tones. He was unbelievable, graceful, and soulful. He was smooth. His notes floated effortlessly.

We were captivated by this champion of music. It was like Marvin Gaye or Luther Vandross had been reincarnated and was living in the cold streets of the Chi. We were blown away, thankful, inspired, overwhelmed, in complete awe of his majestic gift. Raymond had the voice of an angel.

Tarrey and I both knew that he would lift the Rituals crowd the same way he lifted us. Without any hesitation we asked him if he would come inside with us to share his talent. We begged him.

"Oh, I don't know, man. They don't want me in there," Raymond replied.

Based on his appearance, I understood his hesitancy. Honestly, I didn't know how folks would respond to him walking into the door, but I knew that they would be amazed if Raymond had the opportunity to sing.

We kept telling him that it would be all right, and after he contemplated for a few more minutes, we finally convinced him to come in. As soon as we walked in the door, folks turned up their noses and cleared a path. The shock they wore on their faces was expected, but at the same time, it hurt to see their open distaste.

The questions rang:

"What the hell is he doing in here?"

"Why did you bring him in here?"

I knew it would be a battle. Prepared for the onslaught, I told those who asked that he was cool. "Chill out, man! He's with me."

Not wanting Raymond to be pushed out by the comments, his discomfort, or lack of confidence, I rushed him to a seat that would be in my sightline from the stage. Once I got him situated, I headed to the stage and started the show, keeping my eye on him, making sure that he was fine.

"And the church says . . ."

"AIGHT!"

"And the church says . . ."

"AIGHT!!"

"Are y'all ready for the show?!

[The crowd applauded, hooting and hollering.]

I hope y'all ready 'cause we have a very, very special show for you
    tonight!
I know it's been a long week,
But tonight we're going to relieve some of that stress,
And kick the week off right . . .
So if you're ready,
Put those hands together,
Make some noise,
    Buckle up,
    Put your seat belts on,
And get ready for this ride!!
The first poet to the mic is . . .
And the church says!"

"AIGHT!"

The show got rolling. The energy felt great. The band was rocking,
and as always, the poets were destroying the mic in the best way possible. It was another classic Rituals evening.

In between every act, I made sure to see if Raymond needed anything.
He told me that he didn't drink anymore, so I brought him some juice.
When I brought it to him, I noticed that the people around him didn't
look comfortable. Folks scooted away, wincing at his aroma, giving dirty
looks, and isolating him. It was evident that their discomfort made Raymond more skeptical about being there. Noticing this, I wanted to hurry
up and bring him up, but knew it had to be at the right time.

Midway thru the first half of the show, the spot was packed. It was
ridiculous that night. Standing room only. The time was now! I went
up, manned the mic after one of the poets performed, and addressed
the crowd:

"Give it up, Give it up, Give it up!
Ooohh weee . . .
I told y'all we had some heat for y'all tonight.
When it's 10 below when the wind blow,
This is that under the covers with your lover heat!
Uh-oh, she's giving her guy the look.
I think some babies are go' be made tonight!
Hahaha!!
And the church says!"

"AIGHT!"

"Aight, at this time I want to bring up a VERY, VERY, VERY special
    guest.
In all my years, I've never heard anyone as amazing as this individual.
I recently met him, and *in seconds*, he changed my life.
Now, I had to beg him to come in here, but I'm so glad he did.
I know he'll touch your soul the same way he touched mine.
So, I need y'all to give him a VERY, VERY, VERY warm round of
    applause.
I need y'all to make some noise!
Clap your hands, stomp your feet, hit a neighbor!
Well don't hit a neighbor, but give it up for one of GOD's gifts.
Give it up for a man who possesses the voice of an angel.
Make some noise for RAYMONDDD!!!"

As Mark Stampley and his band kicked in, it was clear that this was
by far my best intro that night. The energy was electric! You would have
thought Michael Jackson was coming to the stage. The crowd clapped,
screamed, and hollered, looking around to see who was possibly going
to stand up after an intro like that. Then Raymond appeared.

A wave of shock consumed the room, faces turning toward each other, puzzled by the mysterious reversal of who they were expecting to see up there on stage. With his smile as his shield, Raymond slowly, nervously, made his way to center stage. When Raymond reached me, I gave him the mic, shook his hand, and told him, "Do your thang!"

Raymond stood in front of the mic. Timid at first, he looked out into the crowd and then said, "What's up?!" Like most performers he'd watched before him, he talked to Mark Stampley about what music he wanted, and Mark issued orders to the rest of the band. The room began to fall into the magic of the musical groove.

As soon as the music kicked in, I could tell that Raymond was a lot more relaxed. The music gave him courage. Feeling good, he jumped into the song, throwing his notes like feathered darts. Hearts were the target, and he was hitting all bull's-eyes. Line after line, note after note, Raymond worked the crowd with charisma and vocal precision. He was doing his thang! He sang his heart out! Man, he was amaazzingg! Based on the wild, eruptive reactions from the crowd during his performance, it was clear that no one wanted this flow to stop. No one!

The band followed his accents and crescendos until his magical performance sadly came to an end. When it did, man, I wish you could have been there to see what I saw. This once discriminative crowd, who had turned their noses up to him, rose to their feet and gave Raymond the proudest standing ovation I've ever seen! *Everybody* in that packed room stood up and clapped on and on and on. Raymond, with an even bigger smile on his face, stood there, center stage, absorbing this special love. You could tell that his spirit was lifted. You could see his joy grow.

As I walked back to the stage, I was proud of us all that night. I took the mic, put my arm over his shoulder, and addressed the crowd . . .

"AND THE CHURCH SAYS . . ."

"AIIIGGHHHTTT!!!"

"Please, please, please,
Give another round of applause for Raymond!!!
Give it up for Raymond y'all!!!
This is an angel right here . . .
An angel!!"

Wanting to extend our love, we got a tip bucket from the bar and passed it around for Raymond. In a few short minutes, we raised close to $140. Impressed by the generosity, I rushed over to give the money to Raymond. He was already overwhelmed by the love being received, and he wasn't looking for anything else in return. He was so humbled by the moment. When I finally handed him the money, he lit up even more. He tried turning it down, but I insisted that he take it. I kept telling him that he deserved it and so much more. I told him that everyone wanted him to have it. He gave a huge sigh of relief and thanked me over and over again. He told me he would now have enough money for a haircut, food, and shelter. Knowing that absolutely warmed my heart.

The next week Raymond decided to come back down to Rituals. When he walked up, I almost didn't recognize him. He had on newer clothes, he was cleaned up, and, yes, he had had a haircut. Just like the week before, he thanked Tarrey and me over and over again for inviting him in. He told us that after getting his haircut, he went to his interview, and he got the job. He also told us that he found a place to stay. Wow!

I felt like I had made a difference. I felt like I had helped someone with their life! I felt like I had changed the world, even if it was just a little bit! That's what it was all about, that feeling! It was a testament to the power of reciprocity. His presence, his gifts, and his kindness were a blessing to me as much as my helping was a blessing to him.

DEAR FATHER

I realized how important it is to help one another in times of need, despite what their appearances may be. After all, blessings come our way in all sorts of shapes, colors, and sizes.

To see without eyes is a gift,
Our hearts become braille,
The scales melt,
Lightning strikes,
Connections are electric,
The nature of our currents flow strong,
Foundations firm up,
New light shines,
Seeds sprout,
It feels like spring,
Again . . .
We find the thresholds of new seasons,
Hidden reasons to our lives are revealed,
Sealed with love,
Bordered by the courage to dance with chance,
We find new meanings,
We begin to face the fear of what you once didn't know,
Trusting your spirit more than your eyes,
Feeling more alive,
Complementing what naturally yearns inside,
As you dive in,
Touch,
And are warmed,
By the texture of soul.

TRUE ALARM

One day I got a message from my moms. Not ever one to ignore her messages, I called her right back. She asked me to come home after work 'cause she needed to talk. It sounded serious. When I got there she didn't beat around the bush. She sat me down and told me that she got a call about my dad, saying that he was pretty sick and may not make it. She suggested that I go see him in the hospital and that I take Sergio with me.

Damn, I thought. *Sergio.*

My little brother hadn't seen our pops since he was six or seven. I thought about all the pain I had endured and wondered how hard it must have been for him, not having more time to get to know him.

To this day I wish I had done it all differently. I wish I had taken Serg along on that first visit, to Dad's apartment, and seen our dad a hundred times or more before this moment. I was too immature and engulfed by my own feelings. I wasn't proactive enough to consider my brother's feelings . . . I thought there would be plenty of time. I never imagined their reunion would be like this—in a hospital with our dad sick. Even now it fills me with such regret whenever I think about it.

After driving a half hour from our South suburban home, Serg and I arrived at St. Mary's, a hospital on the southwest side of town. Draped in silence, we walked the long white hallways of the hospital. I was scared for Serg—and for myself.

When we finally arrived at the threshold of his room, I took a deep breath and led the way. Only a curtain stood between us and our father. Slowly, I pulled it back to see him peacefully lying in bed. He was half-asleep and very weak looking.

"Hey, Dad," I said.

He looked up slowly, smiled wide, and coolly said, "What's up, man!" His eyes then focused in on Serg, who was now fifteen, a towering six foot two inches tall.

"Sergio?" he said. "Damn, you got tall!"

I didn't know how Sergio felt, but I felt relieved. It was so good to know that Sergio was able to see our father again. The visit was rough, awkward, and thinking about it now is jolting. I'll admit, writing this is hard . . .

Dad and I did most of the talking while Serg just smiled and laughed at his jokes. We stayed for 'bout thirty minutes, and when it was time to go, we both hugged him in his bed and said good-bye for what we thought was the last time. I felt rushed and uncertain, making it difficult to focus on one specific feeling. I was back on the emotional rollercoaster.

As we walked thru the hospital parking lot, I stared off into the darkness of the night. Driving away from the hospital, I asked Sergio how he felt, telling him that he could talk to me if he needed to. He said he was cool, so I left it alone.

I wish I could have conjured up the speech of a lifetime right then and there. I wanted him to know that he wasn't alone on this. But the perfect words escaped me. I didn't want to preach to him either.

The next week I waited around anxiously for the call, thinking my dad was going to pass away any moment. Most of us have been in situations like this, regarding a family member, so you can understand the cliff-hanging anticipation that comes with waiting. Every day my heart was in my throat. My stomach flipped and tumbled. My thoughts drifted. I went numbly thru the daily motions of life, until a call finally did come . . . he was okay and out of danger! Wow, my dad had fought to stay alive. I felt so good! I felt relief like never before. I felt like I had another chance to really build a relationship with my father.

LOVE IS GANGSTA

Relieved as I was about my dad's recovery and return to his home, the world kept spinning, and it was soon back to business as usual: work, shows, kicking it with my guys, and now strictly kicking it with Tarrey. Around the city, and the country, my popularity was growing, and my passion for poetry was transforming into a career. It was gratifying getting my art out there—having my dad and Tarrey to share the success stories with made it that much better.

Tarrey was quickly becoming my best friend. She understood me. She was honest with me. She made me laugh. She made me want to be a better man. I was always one to enjoy playing the field, but I really was swept up by love. She was beyond special, and my instinct knew it. So while most people I knew were settling down, I was on the verge of settling up.

I laugh out loud when folks chuckle and tell me that love is cute. There ain't nothing cute about love. Yes, it's beautiful to have someone to build with.

It's beautiful having someone to confide in.

It's beautiful to have someone's back, especially when that person has yours.

It's beautiful to have someone who has your best interest at heart.

We weren't built to journey thru life alone; that's why it's beautiful to have someone to share the quest with. It's beautiful, but it's far from cute. It's hard work. It's blood, sweat, and tears. It's finding the compassion to laugh after fighting. It's listening when you feel like you haven't been heard. It's the good, the bad, and the ugly. It's heartache and pain, headaches and strain, breakups and makeups. It's picking up someone when you're down. It's apologizing when you realize you've hurt them, when you have made a mistake, when you have misunderstood the other person's intention. It's dropping your pride. It's caring for someone other than yourself. It's protecting what's yours. It's supporting one another's dreams. It's reminding another person of his or her peace when the demons scream. It's doing what needs to be done when you don't feel like doing it.

Love isn't cute . . . it's gangsta!

Tarrey and I met in January 1999. With the success of the Sunday night shows at Rituals, the promoters started another night. To put a twist on what we were doing on Sundays, they started a comedy and soul night on Thursdays. Wanting to support their event, I looked forward to the new night of entertainment. For its opening, they managed to get together a good crowd. Fifty or so people filled the room as the band played for artists and in between the comedy acts. I worked the room, had a drink, talked to different folks, and soaked up the great energy that was pouring off of the stage.

After an hour or so, when I was gearing up to head out to another spot, I was approached by this beautiful young lady named Tarrey Torae. Without hesitation, she told me that she recognized me from hosting on Sundays. She said that she had quit her job earlier that day to pursue what she loved to do, which was singing. She was preparing to go on stage for her first time in life and wanted some familiar faces in the crowd when she went up. The nervousness she was feeling was so obvious—it was the same nervous sensation that I recognized from my first performance. But I couldn't focus on her fear 'cause she had the most magical, hypnotic, story-filled eyes I had ever seen. I couldn't help but feel a very warm, pleasant energy exuding from her aura.

"Of course I'll check you out," I couldn't help but say. "It would be my pleasure."

When she hit the stage, the beauty of her voice complemented her sweet personality. At the same time, her nervousness held her back. She was good, she was soulful, her tone and pitch was soothing, but I could tell she wasn't completely letting go. Occasionally looking at me from the stage she sang her song, and I admired her courage for getting up there. I appreciated the peace heard in her sound, but after her performance, when she asked me what I thought, I told her that she needed to relax and let go so that the obvious potential could shine even brighter. She appreciated the honesty and agreed with me, as she had felt the same thing on stage. Feeling a connection but wanting to play it cool, I thanked her for sharing her gift. She thanked me for hanging around to support her. She cracked a few jokes, showing her humorous side. I cracked a few jokes, showing mine. I hesitantly said good-bye, than I skated out to the next spot.

Months went by, the summer rolled around, and I was busy buzzing thru the city, performing at different events. I went to an Apollo-style competition being hosted by the local radio station WGCI, at a club called the Clique. The Clique isn't around anymore, but back in the day you would see a lot of the top Chicago entertainers there. On any given night, legends like Bernie Mac and R. Kelly might be in the building. This night the competition was the opening for the station's Chanté Moore/Chantay Savage concert, and one of my guys was singing.

The Clique, formerly a warehouse, held over a thousand people that night. Happy to be out, they scattered smiles about the venue. Laughs echoed around me. Folks drank and danced to the music the DJ played. You could hear the anticipation for the show in the conversations circling the room.

The show started, and so did the Apollo-style "boo birds." The critical crowd booed singer after singer after singer off the stage. Hands down, Chicago has got to be the hardest place to perform. Now, I know New York is rough, but the Chi doesn't play. It was so bad that I was actually a lil worried for my boy. I knew he would normally knock 'em out with his performance, but the crowd was so rowdy that I didn't think they would give him a chance. When he did finally go up, they showed him love—he was the only one who didn't get booed off, which gave him a good chance of winning.

After he was done, it was back to the boo business as usual. As quickly as each singer got up on stage, each one was sent running off. Sometimes instead of booing, they would cue the singer's exit by clapping in the middle of a verse. And if that wasn't enough, the crowd started laughing at those who failed to impress them. It was tough. Being a critic myself, I agreed that some of them didn't belong on stage, but being a performer myself, I felt terrible for those who didn't get a fair shake over the loud roars conjured up by this massive crowd.

As the competition came to a close, I figured my guy had it in the bag. That is, until this girl with guns in her lungs hit the mic. I didn't catch her name when the host and comedian, Big Daddy Woo Woo, introduced her, and my bad eyes couldn't really see her face from where I was at the back of the club, only the bright orange of her dress, but my ears caught a piece of heaven when she opened her mouth, like angels had swooped down onto that stage, grabbed the mic, and calmed every beast in that crowd with the sweetest hymn ever heard.

Girlfriend tore the roof off and the walls down!

The crowd went nuts, giving her hoops, hollers, and eventually a standing ovation, which was very, very rare in the Clique, or Chicago, for that matter. Everyone was on their feet, and I was in the back clapping up a storm for this young Aretha-style soul singer who could hold a note longer than any liar could hold on to their story. I was so impressed. I mean, really impressed. I was blown away!

After everyone performed, they let the crowd choose the winner, and of course the lady phenom in orange stole the show. My guy made his way to the back of the crowd. We decided to skip the rest of the show and dip to another event. On the way out, to my surprise, I bumped into Tarrey. Since our first introduction at Rituals months ago, we had run into each other a few times, but now there was something different about her. She was still sweet, still cool, still beautiful, but she was beaming with a new sense of confidence.

"Wait a minute!" I looked her up and down, checking out her outfit, realizing it was the same orange dress worn by the angel who had torn down the stage and raised the roof. "That was you up there singing?!"

"Yeah!" she said, still glowing from her performance.

"Damn, I can't believe that was you!" I couldn't believe that the same shy girl from lil ole Rituals rocked the gargantuan Clique the way she did. I was shook up. I had already caught feelings for her, but I loved the fact that she had the ability to inspire me.

Hello, your fineness.

Over the next few months, our relationship took off. After a host of phone calls lasting into the night, it was obvious that we had a lot in common. It was obvious that it was easy to talk to one another. We supported one another at our events. We loved the same movies. We had the same beliefs. We both had big, big dreams. We shared the commonality of caring for others. We had a deep affection for our families. We never argued. We spent plenty of beautiful nights together. Our time together was easy. It was smooth. It was fun.

When I gaze at her,
I am amazed by her,
And the glow that she supplies to the atmosphere,
A mere whisper of her voice tickles my inner ear,
I laugh and then look into her eyes as her penetrative spirit appears,
In attempt to sickle any of my fears,
My soul cheers every time she is drawn near,
Because I can hear the melody of her heart . . .
She – is,
the – true,
de –fi,
ni – tion,
of – art.
From the start I knew that I was being kidnapped by an angel,
I have fallen,
Although my feelings and my emotions have "rised" to the occasion,
Only to have become tangled in her angelic wings,
When she sings,
She brings me joy that is healing to every broken womb that keeps
   me suffering,
I never told her,
But one day I kissed her soul because the lips of her aura was
   puckering,
She keeps my heart fluttering,

With every stride that she takes,
She makes my mind hard so love to her thoughts is what I wish
    to make,
You can ship me to the depths of space,
And I'll still be able to picture her face in my fantasies,
As I become the light that caresses the galaxies within her shadow.
For her I would go to battle,
And defend the radiation that her smile supplies to the universe.
If I could sing,
I would echo words about her beauty within a verse.
Being sure to let her know,
That my inking can't even describe a mere inkling of what she's worth,
I'm thinking...
When they say that birth is a miracle,
They must mean that she was the first to stroll the earth and converse
    with the breeze,
I mourn in the eves when I cannot split her atoms,
Bushels of ripe apples, pears, and peaches,
Can't compare to the sweetness that grapples on to her temple.
I find myself getting drunk from the ripples of her sculpted structure,
This enchantress ruptures essence that orbits the rings of elegance,
She is the empress that equates eloquence.
She is exquisite.
Egyptians worship her image,
And describe her as a modest goddess.
I'm being completely honest.
This miss is a myth.
Her presence is a gift wrapped in soulful wishes.
She's the Creator's little princess,
Daddy's little girl,
She's sunshine for the world,

Moonlight for the night,
She is the star in the movie of life,
With Cleopatra playing her stunt double . . .
Double.
If you placed this rose in the middle of junk and rubble,
You would swear it was a garden.
From this paradise I wish not to be pardoned,
My guard I'm disarming,
'Cause I've fallen in like,
It feels so right,
I need her in my life,
Because last night,
We made the moon cry.

After years of dating, after years of living together, after plenty of good times and the struggles of the bad times, after the breakups and the getting-back-togethers, after working together, after dreaming together, I prayed and asked God for protection. The answer I received in return was, "I sent you her." She was my gift, my joy, my best friend. She supported me, and she protected me the same way I supported and protected her.

So, on April 3, 2005, in front of a packed house of Chicagoans who had come out to support her at a show we had put together, I performed "Moon Cry," turned to her, and got on bended knee.

"Tarrey Torae," I asked, "will you spend the rest of your life with me?"

"Yes," she said, and my spirit rejoiced at the growth that I knew we would attain together. Five months later, in front of close to one thousand people (we had a lot of wedding crashers), we exchanged our vows and began our journey as husband and wife.

Aww, that's so . . . gangsta!

THIS IS WHAT IT SOUNDS LIKE WHEN LOVE CRIES

On November 15, 1999, I was out keeping things moving, bouncing from one spot in the city to the next, when my moms messaged me. I called her back right away, and when she picked up, she kept it short, asking me to come home as soon as I could. It sounded urgent, so I dropped everything and raced out to the burbs. Damn, what was it? As upset as she sounded, she wouldn't tell me over the phone.

She grabbed me as soon as I rushed thru the door and sat me down in my room so we could talk. She took a deep breath, looked me in the eyes, and with an unfamiliar calmness in her voice, she told me that she got a call earlier about my father. *Dad?* I thought. *Man, is he sick again? Is he okay?* But before I could bombard her with questions, she swiftly continued, saying that my father, her ex-husband and the love of her life, had been walking down the street on his way to the store . . . had a heart attack . . . and then died.

In the time found between a blink of an eye, my entire soul shattered.

"*Nooooooo*!!!" I wailed. Not my dad!!!

I couldn't believe it. My dad was gone. I couldn't take it. I was in so much pain, and all I could do was cry.

After pouring out my soul, I needed some air. I knew there was only one place where I could find the right combination of love and affection—I headed to Tarrey's on the South Side. The drive to her house was so hard. The waves of pain hit me over and over again. By the time I got there, I was so drained and distraught that when she came to the door, I quietly walked in and headed straight to her bedroom.

Thinking about my dad's death was difficult, but saying it aloud was even harder. Not being able to let go of the words, I pulled her close and hugged her tight. Still not wanting to believe it, I laid my head on her shoulder, took the same deep breath my mother had taken earlier, and with all the reluctance in the world I told her that my father had died.

The news overwhelmed Tarrey. Besides my mother, she was the only one I had fully confided in about my father. She understood, and because of that she held me tighter, squeezing life back into me. Repeatedly she comforted me with her words as her shoulder caught my tears. Like an angel sent to help, she held me in her arms until I eventually fell asleep.

A few nights later, still reeling from the news of my dad's death, I needed to get away. I headed to a spot my dad used to take me to when I was a shorty, the South Side's Rainbow Beach. It was a place that bottled good memories when it came to my dad.

There along Lake Michigan I was reminded of those summer days that we spent flying kites and throwing the Frisbee . . . I was reminded of the joy we found watching the serenity of this massive body of water together . . . I was reminded of my dad's big smile and the face of my older brother as we romped thru the sand . . . I was reminded of the laughter and splashing in the cool shallows of the lake . . . I was reminded of the unconditional joy shared between a father and his sons.

It was the perfect place to find some sense of healing and understanding. It was the perfect place to connect with my dad.

At one point a row of giant rocks stretches one hundred yards or more from the beach out into Lake Michigan. Having always felt a very deep connection to water, I decided to carefully climb from rock to rock in hopes that my low spirits would be lifted. When I reached the end, the last rock became my welcome mat before this small ocean in front of me. I found the driest spot and sat down.

The Chicago winter air was brutally cold, but the sky was clear and beautiful. As I overlooked the night and the lake, as the stars danced like watery reflections, putting me in a trance, reminding me that I was a speck within an infinite nightscape, I finally began to feel peace. I put down my guard. I let my mind settle on my father. I sat in that cold and quietly watched for more than an hour, finding a new level of calm with every passing minute.

My soul opened, and my eyes rained tears, uniting with the rocks underneath and the lake around me.

I didn't feel alone out there. I wasn't alone. I talked to the stars and the moon, and at some point in my conversation with the night, I heard my father speak back to me:

"Jimmy, I'm alright. I'm alright!"

His clear and strong voice sent electricity thru my entire body, starting at my heart. Grateful for being allowed to feel and hear his presence, I repeated to the night sky, "I love you so much, Dad. I *love you so much!*"

I sat there until I couldn't bear the cold any longer. I made a beeline for the beach where I found a stick and wrote my father's name in the sand close to the shoreline: James Ivy Richardson Sr. After his name I tagged the sand with the classic sentiment RIP and then stood there watching as the lake's waves slowly washed his name from the earth. I watched, prayed, and confided to the spirits until his name had disappeared. I took one last look to the sky and the lake, wiped the tears from my face, turned, and headed back to my car.

GOOD-BYE, DAD

My dad's older sister, Aunt Christine, was left with the responsibility of planning her baby brother's funeral services. They had already lost their older brother back in 1983. I can only imagine what it was like having the last of her siblings pass away. But knowing she held a duty to her brother, she wouldn't let the pain stop her. She pressed on and made all the arrangements for the upcoming service. I admired her strength, and she was a great example of how to hold yourself together for the sake of others. Her resilience showed me that I needed to warrior thru this moment, no matter how difficult. My auntie had always been a sweetheart, showering us with love, but it was something special witnessing the tenacity of her power. It gave me strength and inspiration during a very weak moment in my life.

So when she asked me to write a poem for the funeral that coming Saturday, I couldn't say no. It was an honor. It was an honor to represent her. It was an honor to represent my mother and my brothers. It was an honor to represent my family.

It was an honor to stand as a son, a young man, and pay tribute to my dad. I wanted to let him know what I felt. I wanted the world to know what I felt.

The next day, with the voice of my father at the lake still ringing in my ears, I sat down in my room and let my instincts flow. I wrote a poem for my father.

THE MAN I WAS

You know,
I tried being strong,
But I can't help but hurt.
Even though I know the Lord has lifted the curse,
My entire world has been reversed.
Rewinding my mind to our good times together,
Best friends forever,
That would fly kites in the summer and make snowmen in snowy
    weather.
Your soul can't be measured,
You brought pleasure to most that were around you.
You made mistakes, but I forgive you.
You helped create me, so part of me lives for you.
A part of my soul I give to you,
Thru prayer I will build with you.
I feel that I have a lot to do,
So I'll be able to correct some of the mistakes that were made.
When you cared for Virgil, love is what you gave,
When you created me and Sergio, love is what you made,
And now that love will be portrayed,
As we look above to you,

DEAR FATHER

Calling on you when we are in need of assistance,
Staying conscious of your spiritual existence.
I know you were heaven-sent,
Which is why your spiritual body was torn from your physical,
And sent back to heaven,
Sent back home,
Your being will never again be alone,
Because you are now in a better place,
Where your heart will be able to beat at a better pace.
Yes, you're now free,
And I know, because last night I could feel you walking with me,
Last night,
I know you were praying with me as I carved your name in the sand,
So the lake could wash it from the land.
Last night,
For the first time you didn't seem so far.
I know you were with me as I conversed with the water, the moon,
    and stars.
Last night,
I know that you were with me as I asked the Creator to look over you,
I know you heard me when I told you that I loved you.
I know,
Because last night,
While I sat on the lake,
In tears,
With a prayer falling off of my tongue . . .
You spoke to me and said,
"Jimmy, I'm all right. I'm all right!
Tell everyone that I'm all right . . ."
So to Christine, he thanks you and loves you,
To Pam, he said, "I never stopped loving you,"

To Virgil and Sergio he said,
"I hope that the two of you can find it in your hearts to forgive me,
Because I love you two very much!"
And your grandmother is telling me to tell you that she loves you
   too . . ."
So to James Ivy Richardson Sr.,
Jim Richards,
Dad,
I would like to say, rest in peace,
And I love you,
I love you,

I Love You!!!

When my family and I arrived for my dad's services, I greeted everyone in a daze. I was grateful to see loving faces there in support— family members, Tarrey, friends, and others—but I found myself being short with everyone. I couldn't find the energy to converse, so I quickly walked into the sanctuary, to my father.

Immediately my eyes fixed themselves on the casket. I slowly walked toward my dad, with each step growing heavier then the last. I wished to turn back the hands of time, but I couldn't. I was forced to deal with this moment. I was left to take on my fear and regret.

When I arrived at the foot of his casket, I was scared to gaze upon his face . . . I didn't have to, but I did. I looked at my father lying there stiff and still. My God, where had the life gone? I never imagined him looking like this. I never imagined seeing him spiritless, being nothing more than a human shell. I never imagined not being able to speak to him again.

I couldn't handle looking at his lifeless body. Overwhelmed, I quickly turned around to head out of the room, quietly passed friends and family to the downstairs bathroom. I couldn't move fast enough. As soon as I was in a stall, I started to break down . . . again. My tears fell like a waterfall. I couldn't pull the toilet paper off of the roll quickly enough. Mucus stuffed my nose. I tried to find understanding, but I was lost in misery. That's when I heard someone walk into the bathroom.

"Jimmy, you all right in there?" It was Sergio. He had followed me down.

"Yeah," I said very unconvincingly.

Not believing the weak response, Serg pushed the cracked door open to see his big brother broken down, leaning on the stall, bawling out of control.

I wasn't looking at him but could feel him step closer, and he put his arms around me and said, "It's all right, Jimmy. He knew that you loved him. And he loved you too."

His sincerity shook me up even more. There I was, being consoled by my little brother. It should be the other way around. It should've been the big brother protecting the little brother, the way I tried to do when we were younger. I wished that was the way it would have been, but it was hitting me so hard. I was hurt. The pain was passionate. It was alive. At the same time, Serg knew exactly what I was thinking, and what he said helped me tremendously. I heard him loud and clear. I took some deep breaths and got it together, and then we headed back upstairs . . . together.

The preacher started the service, but I didn't like the idea of some man who didn't know my father talking about him. It felt so impersonal. It didn't feel genuine. I was sidetracked by these thoughts until he called me to come up.

Since my incident in the bathroom, I had somewhat held myself together. Now that it was time for me to speak, I was in tears and unable to stand up. I wanted to be strong for my mother and my family. I wanted to be strong for my father. I heard someone say, "You can do this, James!" The words rang loudly in my head. I knew I couldn't live with the regret of not speaking for my father and everyone affected by his passing. I needed to get the piece off of my chest.

I gathered myself and headed to the podium. My tears clouded my eyes and dripped onto the page, making it hard to read the poem. At first, I read the piece with hesitation in my heart. I was choked up. My words were muffled. But then I read with all that I had. I cried out line after line till I was done. When I finished, I grabbed my pad and damn near ran to my mother, who was sitting a few rows from the front. When I got to her, I fell to the neighboring seat, wrapped my arms around her, and said, "He told me to tell you that he never stopped loving you! He said he never stopped loving you!!" We held each other as our somber tears of disappointment, regret, and love danced together.

The preacher wrapped up the services and gave everyone directions to the cemetery. Before leaving, I thanked my cuz Julia for telling me to forgive my father. I thanked her for telling me to let go of the past. I told her I didn't know what I would have done, if he'd passed without me having a chance to forgive. I told her that I was happy I was able to see and tell him that I loved him. Warm and full of love, she hugged me and told me that that is what family is for. I agreed. That is what family is for. We are put here to lift each other up and remind one another of our beauty and pride. We are put together to help guide one another thru the challenges of life.

Embracing the lesson, I headed over to the cemetery to watch my father's body be put into its final resting place. Everyone gathered at the burial site, folks said their final good-byes, my father's casket was lowered into the ground, the preacher said one final prayer. I threw a little white flower onto his casket.

"Good-bye, Dad."

He was gone . . . my father was gone.

FORGIVENESS IS REMEMBERING TO FORGIVE AGAIN

Our emotions are real. Our feelings are real. Some memories aren't erased by time. As human beings we naturally and often reflect on our past. We think back to certain times. Smells, colors, the sound of someone's laugh, songs, movies, reruns of old shows, shifts in the weather, dates on the calendar, holidays, passing cars, certain foods, landmarks throughout the city all remind us of different points in our lives. Our memories spark, becoming our personal time machine, transporting us back. These memories are at times happy, draping us with joy. At other times they are hard or hurtful, reminding us of the pain we once felt. We never know when exactly something in our life will trigger these feelings.

For these moments that are hard, these times when past scars reappear, it becomes pertinent that we find ways to control the weight of these feelings. Our joy deserves our protection. We deserve to be happy. Isn't that why we're here? When we reflect on the moments that taught us valuable lessons, we face a natural challenge to separate the emotion that we felt at that time from current emotions. The textures of our memories are layered with the elements of that time. We remember what the weather was like. We remember what we had on. We remember where we were coming from and where we were headed. We know who was there and who said what. We remember the causes that shifted the course of the situation. We remember the moments falling like dominos. The habits of our thought patterns place us right back in the moment, as if we were living it all for the first time.

When it comes to dealing with these hard times that were caused by others, especially when it's caused by those closest to us, it's a journey to find it in our hearts to forgive. Words are thrown at us that forever stick to our spirits. Hateful things are said that echo in our minds. We begin to believe the lies, the judgmental acts, and the doubts of others. We become what others think until we can forgive and let it go. But letting go is hard. We lose precious time trying to figure out why so and so would do this to us. *What did I ever do to him? Why would she do that to me?* Those are the questions that are bounced between the pain in our hearts and the logic in our minds. We just want to understand. But trying to understand may be our biggest crime. *Tarrey once told me, "What others think about you is none of your business."*

I believe that's true. It isn't any of my business what you think. Everything isn't meant for me to understand. What you think about me is your opinion—knowing that it's important that we don't take things so personally. What I think about me is mine, my business. Trying to understand why you don't see things the way I do is a waste of time. And often we miss out on the next opportunities trying to figure out the ones behind us.

When my cuz told me that I needed to forgive to release myself of the heavy pain I was experiencing, I realized that forgiveness starts in the heart. It starts with creating the life you want for yourself. Who are you really and what does that include? Does your true self want to stay in a place of anger, rage, sadness, or misery? Do you love living in that state? Is it your dream to remain in the shadows of depressing times or do you want to dance in the sun? Who are you?

We forget to take the time to consider what may have pushed people to the point they are at. We don't think about the hurt or traumas they may have encountered. I've found that most people don't want to worry others with their problems. Some are ashamed of what they've been thru. Some are guided by pride that won't allow them to touch on certain feelings. Folks become very guarded not knowing how to cope with their pain. Whatever the case may be, people are imperfect human beings. We all make mistakes. We've all been hurt.

Pain can intoxicate us like most drugs, causing us to do things and say things that we didn't really mean. We've all done it. We've all felt the guilt and regret of the negativities we've spewed out. We've all been pushed by our anger. We've all made off-balance decisions that we feel remorseful about later. When we calm down, we clearly see everything that we could have done differently. We know that we weren't in our right minds. We know we weren't our true selves. We know our actions didn't meet our intentions.

Becoming aware of who you are, remembering to have compassion for others, and not taking things personally still presents a challenge when it comes to forgiving. Forgiveness is an exercise. The act of forgiving becomes physical. It becomes a physical task. It's heavy and it's hard, like pushing two-ton stones uphill. Finding the strength and the courage to clean the slate of your own newly formed judgments is hard, but it's something that you are capable of doing. You have the power to let go. You have the ability to exercise your love.

When you remove the negative emotions.

When you let go of the anger.

When you let go of the hate.

When you let go of the fear.

When you let go of feeling disappointed.

When you let go of expectation.

When you let go of your self-pity.

When you stop feeling sorry for yourself.

When you muscle up and let go, you take back your freedom that heartache locked away.

You were put here for a reason. It's important that you remember your significance and not let anyone interrupt your walk. I know my path has been interrupted time and time again 'cause I allowed the pain of others to hurt me. Hurt people hurt people, and we've all been hurt. We've all hurt someone we've loved. We've all hurt someone we haven't known. But my intention is never to hurt anyone. And I'm sure my dad's intention wasn't to hurt me. His actions may not have matched that but neither have my imperfect acts toward others.

Like the saying goes, "Don't judge the speck in my eye without seeing the log in yours." We all make mistakes. We all will make more. The key is not to judge but to focus on your purpose. Despite what anyone may have done in the past, you're still standing. You're still able to move forward in your life. You are still awarded with the ability to dream, create, and find happiness. But in order for us to find these joys, we have to forgive. And when the mechanics of our mind flash back to yesteryear, we have to remember that . . .

Forgiveness
Is
REMEMBERING
To forgive again,
And again,
And again,
And . . .

PART III

POWER

...NG THAT WAS LOST. AND THEY WOULD MAKE ME

...AND GIGGLE. AND ~~MY BOY~~ EVEN TAUGHT ME HOW TO

SO ...L ⊙ I COULD MAKE THE TEAM. AND I DID. I

...T I WOULD DIE WITHOUT YOU BUT ~~TO~~ MY BOYS MADE   ROME, TODD, DRE, & ERIC

...THAT I LIVED. AND WAS NEVER ~~MORE~~ SAD. THEY EVE...

...ME THERE DAD'S, MR. KEMP, MR. WHITAKER, MR. C...   THEY WE WE WROTE THERE DADS

...R. MASANOS BECAME ~~MY DAD~~ MY COOL DADDYS. BUT   PRICE

...ITTLE BOY IN ME STILL WANTS HIS DADDY. BAD

...LL LIKE A SCARED LIL BOY AFRAID TO BECOME A

...UT IM READY. ITS TIME, ITS TIME TO SHINE. ITS   I THINK

...TO SHINE AND ...TO SHINE AND

...INE SO I ...STAND LET MY SOUL

...ITS TIME TO STAND AS A MAN ON MY OWN ~~OR~~ TWO.

~~. CAUSE ALL I EVER WANTED WAS TO MAKE YOU AND~~

~~PROUD.~~ JUST LIKE YOU USE TO DO BEFORE THOSE

...B STARTED HAUNTING YOU. ITS TIME. CAUSE ALL I

...WANTED TO DO WAS MAKE YOU AND ME PROUD. AN...

...DER IF YOU ARE, I WONDER IF YOU KNOW, I WA...

...KNOW THAT GOD GAVE ME A GIFT. I WONDER

...KNOW ABOUT THE SPIRITS ~~I~~ THAT I LIFT. I WONDER

...KNOW THAT I TOUCH PEOPLE WITH MY WORDS.

...IF YOU KNOW

...F INSPIRE ACTION WITH MY VERBS. I WONDER IF YO...

...HAT YOU BABY BOY DID A SHOW THAT AIRED FOR MILLIONS

...ON HBO. AND THAT HARD ASS NEW YORK CROWD GAV...   ACTUA

...STANDING O. DID YOU KNOW. I KNOW YOU KNOW. I

...IMA BE THE BEST JUST LIKE YOU WANTED TO BE WATCH IN...

...P. AND JUST IN CASE YOU DIDN'T IM A SCREAM

LOVE THAT WAS LOST. AND THEY WOULD MAKE M—
UGH AND GIGGLE. AND ~~MY BOY~~ EVEN TAUGHT ME HOW TO
BBLE ⊙ SO I COULD MAKE THE TEAM. AND I DID.
REHT I WOULD DIE WITHOUT YOU BUT ~~TO~~ ROME, TODD, DRE, ZEK H
MY BOYS MA—
E THAT I LIVED. AND WAS NEVER ~~MAD~~ SAD. THEY ⊙
E ME THERE DAD'S. THEY LET ME ABOUT THERE DADS MR. KEMP. MR. WHITAKER. MR—
MR. ~~HASKINS~~ PRICE BECAME MY DADS. MY COOL DADDYS. B
LITTLE BOY IN ME STILL WANTS HIS DADDY. B
FELL LIKE A SCARED LIL BOY AFRAID TO BECOME A
⊙ BUT ,THINK IM READY. ITS TIME. ITS TIME TO SHINE. H
⊙ TO SHINE AND GET MINE. ITS TIME TO SHINE AND
MINE SO I CAN ~~EASE~~ MY MIND AND LET MY SO
ITS TIME TO STAND AS A MAN ON MY OWN ~~TOO~~ THE
UB. ~~CAUSE ALL I EVER WANTED WAS TO MAKE YOU~~
~~PROUD.~~ JUST LIKE YOU USE TO DO BEFORE THO
OWS STARTED HAUNTING YOU. ITS TIME. CAUSE ALL I
R WANTED TO DO WAS MAKE YOU AND ME PROUD. ⊙
ONDER IF YOU ARE. I WONDER IF YOU KNOW. I
YOU KNOW THAT GOD GAVE ME A GIFT. I WON
YOU KNOW ABOUT THE SPIRITS THAT I LIFT. I WOND
OU KNOW THAT I TOUCH PEOPLE WITH MY WORDS
DER IF YOU KNOW
⊙ I INSPIRE ACTION WITH MY VERBS. I WONDER IF
THAT YOU BABY BOY DID A SHOW THAT AIRED FOR MILLIO
E ON HBO. AND THAT HARD ASS NEW YORK CROWD ACT
A STANDING O. DID YOU KNOW. I KNOW YOU KNOW. I
⊙ IMA BE THE BEST JUST LIKE YOU WANTED TO BE WHICH
⊙ AND JUST IN CASE YOU DIDNT IM A SLEEP

JIM RICHARDS' BAG

One of the toughest parts about my dad's passing was having the responsibility of helping clean out his apartment. I didn't want to deal with this kind of burden, but when Aunt Christine called and asked for my help, I knew I couldn't leave her to do it on her own. It was only days after my dad, her brother, left the graces of this world, and it had to be done before there were any issues or additional charges from the landlord. Not wanting to procrastinate, my aunt and Uncle Charles drove down from Milwaukee, and I headed over to my dad's to meet up with them.

There I was, back at the doorstep of my reunion with my dad, when I walked up those stairs and fearfully pushed the black rectangular doorbell, not knowing what to expect, his brown door slowly opening to reveal an old man of a father whom I had missed like life itself.

This time, he wasn't there to greet me. Instead, here I was standing alone, overwhelmed with the significance of that past memory. It felt so odd, like I was in *The Twilight Zone*. It didn't seem right that he wasn't here to say, "Hey, son." Hearing those two simple words would have felt like heaven in that moment, but the empty space filling the doorway felt like hell instead. I was furious and regretful for not being more proactive after we had reconnected.

Why hadn't I called? Why didn't he call? Gripped by my guilt, I zoned out, spaced out. I felt lost, unsure of what to make of this madness... this sadness.

When I got inside, my aunt and uncle were already handling the strain of the task. They had boxes handy for my dad's belongings, a broom and dustpan handy for sweeping up, and a roll of Hefty bags handy for everything else. In a state of grief, Auntie was working steadily to handle the toughness of the moment.

Not wanting this to last any longer than it had to, I jumped right in and began clearing things out. The one-bedroom apartment was small, and my dad didn't have many belongings, making the cleanup easier than expected. There were clothes, some pictures, address books, a few lamps, and other little knickknacks. My aunt told me I could take whatever I wanted. This was my inheritance, my legacy. My dad had worked his whole life, but there weren't many signs of that. I could sense the magnitude of loneliness he must have felt. I wished I had been there for him.

As we cleaned, I came across things that painted a clearer picture of who my dad was. Every youthful photo or image of him or his family made me smile. In each shot I could see the love and pride. I could see his joy, his personality shining thru. His clothes were another sign of that. The old-school gear, the nylon shirts, the turtlenecks, the patterned ties, the hard-bottomed shoes, the bell-bottomed slacks—all were significant of his generation's style, which he had plenty of.

Among the small fortune in memories there was one thing that stood out, a burnt-orange leather satchel with a metal clasp and shoulder strap. The midsize bag was cool and looked like something I would rock myself. Curious to see what was inside this 80s throwback, I unlatched the hook, caught a whiff of that classic cowhide smell, and lifted the flap.

The inside of the flap was branded with a Motown logo. *Wow, how cool is this? A bag from Motown*, I thought, wondering who might have given him the bag, which of the many stars he might have met in his radio days. Michael, Stevie, Marvin, Diana, Smokey?

I dug into the bag and pulled out a handful of cassette tapes with my dad's handwriting on them, all along the lines of this:

KBWH (Good) 8/9/85 Master–Jim Richards AIRCHECK.

They were some of my dad's work. In the radio world, an aircheck tape is a demo of a disc jockey's voice and talent—commercials, voiceovers, introductions of songs, and other past work—a vocal resumé.

Once upon a time, I created one for myself when I was looking to do some radio work. It made sense he'd have them, but I'd never seen them before, so finding them now was like learning something new about him. To find that I had traveled a similar path as my dad was mind blowing. More important, I had something to remember him by. After years of not hearing his voice, I held tapes that would house his voice forever. I had struck gold. My dad would live on thru his work. Work that he obviously carried with him everywhere he went, another sign of his love for music. All that was left of his career was this bag that he held on to like a photo of a loved one. The years, the hours, the dedication, the dreams, the life passions, and the desire to be great had dwindled down to ten cassette tapes . . . simple samples of my dad's gift.

Burnt-orange,
Leathered,
Scorned by chances lost,
This dream deferred,
Preferred to be heard beyond the belly of this bag.
Over his shoulder he carried his dreams,
But looked over his shoulder and watched his back.
Back when life was ahead of him,
Ahead of him were brick walls that were too tough to break down.
Every person breaks down.
We forget to put the brakes down.
We don't stop,
We go faster,
We crash in the city,
Sleep on our potential.
It could all be so simple,
But we complicate things,
Seasons change but we stay the same.
Different strokes for different folks,
It's sink or swim,
Now that I'm older I get him,
Maybe because I'm related to him,
Standing there with my heritage in hand I related to him,
I jumped in this bag and raced back in time,
Listening to every line,
Every chime,
The smell of old leather engulfed my spirit,
Brought me closer to history,
His gift was written on the walls of his heart,
His voice spoke reflecting his love,
His passion was evident,

Relevance was discovered,
Uncovered by technology,
Recordings that housed this gift,
His presence was felt in each inflection,
Each style that was exercised showed his versatility . . .
He was boxless,
Limitless,
A talent dancing with potential,
Audio credentials that soothed my mental.
My moment was enhanced by this inheritance,
The love and the shortcomings,
Long-term effects affected him,
Haunted by a past that didn't translate into the future he
    dreamed of,
He let the dark side strike him down so he could live on,
He lives on thru this sweet memento . . .
Airchecks that remind me to check the air,
Listen for his voice,
His guidance,
I feel his smile in his style,
I feel his smile in my style,
Flavor that I got honestly,
Honestly I see where I get it from,
A chip off the old block,
An apple of the same seed,
Desires cut from the same creed,
Same cloth,
We're getting chewed on by the same moth,
Battling the same demons,
Working on remembering my confidence, my gifts, my beliefs,

My dreams speak,

SCREAM,

Drowning out the spiked noise,
Our joys will live,
Will heal . . .
We'll build the bridge of this legacy that hate tried to burn down,
You can't burn this down,
From father to son . . . from son to father,
Love lifts us from our falls,
Time and the clarity of your voice speaks volumes,
Letting me know that this amplified love heals all . . .

POETICALLY INCLINED

Becoming an adult, being hit with the responsibilities of maintaining a livelihood and realizing that you have to deal with grownup issues can at times be frustrating as hell. We all have our ups and downs, we all have our challenges, and for me writing became the release I needed when dealing with the strains of stress. Like breathing it became a necessity. It allowed me to scream when there was no one there to listen, when no one wanted to listen, or when I didn't want to weigh someone else down with my problems.

You see, art for the soul is like food for the body; we need it. If we don't eat, we wither away and die. But if we constantly feed on the tensions of life without trimming the fat, we suffer from the side effects of our stressful obesity. We lack energy; we drag, become diseased, depressed with what we've become, leaving us feeling ashamed to look in the mirror. We fall out of love with ourselves, no longer liking what we see. The pain that goes unreleased eats away at us like cancerous cells, dulling our senses and our ability to connect to ourselves and others. We need to cleanse ourselves, wash our bodies and detox our internal systems.

I need that release.
You need that release.
We all need that release.

Poetry is my safety net, my great escape, so I decided to do just that, to escape in the diverse dimensions of my words. I decided to escape to the comfort of my world. I wanted to lose myself, even if it was just for a moment. I desperately needed this break from reality, so I packed up and made a detour to Lake Michigan.

One of my favorite places in the world has always been a manmade peninsula on the South Side of the lake called the Point. Whenever I needed to breathe, whenever I needed to slow down, think, meditate, pray, this is the place where my heart would take me. It's my peace, my piece of the city that calms me down. Looking out onto the water, I'm instantly overtaken by the beauty of God's creation. It's beautiful, a breath of freshwater air that slows me down and helps me focus.

There on the east side of Lake Shore Drive, the water meets a rocky limestone edge. Moving inward you come to a concrete walkway, giant cement blocks also perfect for sitting and lying, and a stony staircase that leads fifteen to twenty feet up to the trees and the city park's paved walkway. The walkway wraps around a huge field. There you'll find folks having picnics, getting married, having cookouts, running, going for walks, flying kites, enjoying their dates, or just hanging out and relaxing. The view of downtown, the skyline, and the lake is priceless. It's perfect.

It's inspirational, and I yearned to be inspired, so I headed there with the quickness. I knew what I was feeling was more than a want.

I needed to express myself the same way I need food, water, and a roof over my head. Expression is my oxygen, and in that moment I needed to breathe. I needed to exhale my hell. I needed to let it all go. So with a pen and pad in my hands, an early sun shining down on me, seagulls soaring thru the sky, and squirrels cautiously hopping by, I did just that. For the next ten minutes, in the center of that field, I walked in circles, pacing, venting, regurgitating every emotion my spirit had been forced to consume, watching the words spill onto the page, as I speed-wrote whatever came to mind. I needed to write.

So I did.

I NEED TO WRITE . . .

I need to sit my black narrow behind down and write.
Yeah, the hustle got me hustlin',
But I'm muscling myself out of time for me,
Well what about me I ask?
What about the stories that I need to tell?
I need to write.
'Cause can't nobody do it for me,
Can't nobody document my inspirations the way I can,
Can't nobody compliment my aspirations the way I can,
ONLY I CAN,
ONLY I CAN,
ONLY I CAN,
So I NEED to write.
I need to gather up some words and write,
I need to gather up some thoughts and write,
I need to write,
'Cause I'm tired of hearing the same ole pieces,
I know y'all tired of hearing the same ole pieces,
'Cause the same ole pieces got the same ole problems,

But I got new problems,
Mo' problems,
Problems have changed,
Problems have rearranged,
This homeless cat asked me for some money,
But got mad at me 'cause I ain't got no spare change.
I need to write.
Me and my girl been arguing,
I need to write!
My boy told me that I need to take it to the next level,
I need to write!
My pops died and it's hard dealing with it,
I need to write!
I know y'all can't wait for the book,
I need to write!
They done stole my hooptie,
I need to write!
The cops said I fit the description,
I need to write!
My little brother got mugged by some grown thug,
I need to write!
You're talking about me behind my back,
I need to write!
I ain't got it no mo'?!
I need to write!
My ex tried to get with my boy,
I need to write!
The weather been actin' offly funny,
I need to write!
It's time to take Jesus off that cross,
I need to write!

Cops killin' brothers,
Cops killin' sistas,
Free Mumia!
I need to write!
Oh, so I'm gay 'cause I don't want to get with you?!
I need to write!
They were taking good care of that lil Cuban boy,
What about the shorties in the projects?
I need to write!
You sayin' I'm bogus cause I didn't come to yo event,
'Cause I was tired,
I need to write!
I distinctly remember asking for six wings with mild sauce,
Why is it I only have four?!
I need to write . . .
I think about writing in third person,
'Cause the first is hurtin',
Life is a job and the verse is workin',
My soul's rehearsing for when the Lord pulls the curtain,
Words are words,
So maybe it's your actions that's doin' the cursin' . . .
I need to write!
Just yesterday it was illegal for me to write,
Where's my pen at?

I NEED TO WRITE!

Live performance of I Need to Write
http://tagr.com/t/V4cJRR

MAKING MOVES IN MUSIC CITY

had never grieved over a parent, so I didn't know I needed to talk about the pain either. I never wanted to be the one springing my problems on others, so I kept things to myself. Time heals all, but every now and then I would find myself lapsing into my sadness.

I missed my dad.

I missed him, but I knew he would want me to keep things moving. Movement was key. I needed to keep going. I loved my city, but with my pain deeply grappled in every element, every turn, everywhere I went, I desperately needed to get away to heal and regroup.

Tarrey and I decided to move to the Ville, Nashville, Music City. When it came to moving, we had a few cities in mind, but I had collaborated with a Nashville producer to create a lot of music for my poetry. The music was refreshing, and after shooting down to the Ville to work with him a few times, I met a manager there who exposed me to some great opportunities. The city seemed to be the perfect place to catch my breath, create, and get a feel for a city other than the Chi. It was a chance to spread my work, meet new people, and get a fresh start. Besides, their Southern winters were like an island hop in comparison to Chicago.

It was tough saying good-bye to Rituals, but I knew it was time to move on to new things. Chicago has always been home, and no matter where I rest my head in this world, it will always be home. It will always be warmly waiting. It was that love that pushed me forward. It's that love that pumps thru me and inspires me to be the best. It was that love that made me want to conquer these ill feelings.

So, we were off.

Over the next year and a half, Nashville proved to be a great decision. Tarrey and I were having our ups and downs in our relationship, but we were both busy doing a lot of shows. We made a great name for ourselves performing with a band we put together. We were performing at all the big festivals. We were writing with different folks around town. We both finished our solo albums. I opened up for one of my biggest inspirations, the late great Gil Scott-Heron. And I miraculously landed an incredible opportunity on *Russell Simmons Presents Def Poetry*.

MY FAITHFUL ROAD
TO DEF POETRY

Faith is a force that forges the tools you'll need to construct the road of your destiny. Yes, there are rules to the road. Every chapter has its ups and downs. Things happen. You just have to know and believe in the power of your energy, your purpose, which will unlock doors that were meant for you and only you to open.

Since I've been on my path of poetry, since I found the courage and will to pursue this discovery, this dream of mine, blessings have fallen into my lap. My keys have miraculously revealed themselves. Opportunity has knocked before I was even conscious of the door. I have found that when you work hard on your loves and passions, the opportunities come. You hear stories of those making it overnight, but what has happened is they have made it their lifelong mission to not give up, and the Universe has complied. The needed energy you desire to make it to the next level is pulled to you. Magically, the muscle for your movement is magnetized to your moment.

You can get in where you fit in,
or you can make room.

While living in Nashville in 2001, my slate was dirtied by messes that seemed unavoidable. At the time I didn't have a job, Tarrey caught her boss going thru her purse and had to leave her job, shows had grown sporadic, at different points our lights and phones had been cut. The stress led us to arguments. And I would have sad, moody moments thinking about my dad being gone.

To top it off, one Monday I received a slew of calls from poets and friends back in Chicago asking me where was I that previous weekend. Apparently *Def Poetry*, a show that I had been hearing Russell Simmons was developing to follow up his infamous *Def Comedy Jam*, had held a competition over the weekend to find poets to represent Chicago. At this point the talk of *Def Poetry* had been going on for a couple of years, and earlier on I had been told that I would be a part of the Chicago show when it landed in town, but when it did, I didn't know anything about it. Most poets in the country were dreaming of an opportunity like this, so hearing the news tore me up. I began beating myself up with guilt.

I was mad at myself for moving to Nashville. I was mad that I had taken myself out of the Chicago scene. I felt that I had missed out on a once-in-a-lifetime opportunity. Yes, I learned that the saying "Out of sight, out of mind" was true. Yes, you have to be present in order to receive your opportunities. Yes, nothing in life is easy, but still, my heart, which was still filled with hope, was hurt.

During this dragging spell, Tarrey's intuition told her it was time to break up the monotony and my slump. One day she reminded me of a ticket voucher she hadn't used from a flight she had changed earlier in the year. She said, "Let's go to LA!" We were tight on money, but by planning ahead we could cover two tickets with the voucher, we had friends to crash with, and we would try to find work to do while we were out there. "Let's Go!"

A couple of weeks later we were set to head out to California, aka the Golden State. Just the thought of the trip relieved some stress, as I was more than ready for the break. Wanting to line up possible gigs, I let Emmit, my manager at the time, know we were taking a trip to Los Angeles. Immediately he said, "You need to hook up with Michelle while you're there."

Months earlier, I had met his friend Michelle, who was a music supervisor for film and television. Michelle loved my poetry and wanted to help us get my work out there, but she said she was having trouble describing to people what exactly it was that I did. We all felt that it would be better to show the people rather than tell them, so when Emmit told her we were on the way, she said, "That's perfect."

And it was perfect. The timing couldn't have been better. The weekend we were in LA "just happened to be" Michelle's birthday weekend, and she was having a barbecue at her house to celebrate. She said a lot of her film friends would be there, and I should perform. I loved the idea. I loved performing. I loved meeting new people. So we were off!

Tarrey and I headed to LA on a Thursday, rented a red Firebird convertible, let our hair blow in the Cali wind, and got to work. Over the next couple of days, we linked up with one of our good friends, Marc "M. Doc" Williams, who had produced and remixed songs for Janet Jackson, Ce-Ce Peniston, Kelly Rowland, Chris Brown, Madonna, and others. Together, Doc, Tarrey, and I wrote and recorded a hot summer song called "Un-Huh." The next day we linked with another good friend and producer named George Claiborne, and Tarrey recorded a beautiful ballad called "Another Love." So far the trip was proving to be perfect.

When Saturday afternoon rolled around, we excitedly headed to Michelle's birthday celebration. We stopped by the liquor store, grabbed a bottle of red Alizé and some flowers for Michelle and made our way to her house up in the Hollywood Hills. When we got there, we parked on her slanted street, fixed our clothes, and walked downhill to her house. Upon our ringing the bell, Michelle opened the door, greeting us with the warmest welcome and the biggest hugs. "*J. Ivy!!* Is this Tarrey?! *Hey, girl!* Welcome, welcome! Come on in!" Right away the love shown made us feel right at home. The smiles were endless.

Michelle and her husband had a beautiful home. From the layout to the furniture to the artwork, the modern abode felt very warm and relaxing. That warmth was easily seen in the forty to fifty people who were already scattered around the house and outside in the backyard. Being that Tarrey and I were two of the three black folks there, we immediately stood out, but since leaving the segregated ways of Chicago, I was learning time and time again that people from different walks of life really could get along.

About an hour later, as the sun was beginning to fall and the moon revealed itself, Michelle asked me if I was ready to perform. More than anxious, I said of course. Michelle gathered everyone's attention, made an announcement, gave me a beautiful introduction, and asked me to take the made up stage area in the middle of the small yard. When I hit the performance area, I cracked a few jokes and then went into my thang, performing "Moon Cry." Tarrey's voice is so soothing and healing, so I asked her to sing her song "Still Will Love You," which was the perfect transition into "Wings."

I still will love you, no matter where you are,
If it's near or far . . .
If you're in Asia or Africa or even North America . . .
Hello . . .

Is there anybody out there?

I got a story to tell . . .

The performance was seamless. It was smooth. It was fun. Tarrey and I inspired one another and after leaving the stage area to the sounding of a thunderous applause, we knew that the audience had been moved as well.

We were showered with compliments and thanked for sharing our art. After leaving our rut behind in Nashville, it was such a good feeling to be standing there on the top of that hill being charged by the joy of others. It was so good to be receiving love from complete strangers so far away from home. It was reinvigorating, giving us hope to push forward, despite the challenges that we were eventually going back to.

The next day, after visiting some more friends, we sadly got on the plane, left the Golden State, and headed back to Nashville. Neither of us wanted to go, but we knew we needed to face our responsibilities, and so we did.

A few days passed, and Michelle called me. She asked if I had ever heard of *Def Poetry*.

"Yeah," I said, "I've been trying to get down with that for a while now!"

"Well, my father was at my party, and he loved you," she said. "He was having lunch yesterday with one of his good-good friends Stan Lathan, who is the director of *Def Poetry*, and told him he needs to check you out." Michelle said Stan called her, and she told Stan, "Oh, J. Ivy! He's great! He's the best!" Stan wanted to see me perform, she said. My jaw dropped to the floor!

After the update, Michelle asked me if I could get back to LA. Knowing money was tight, but confident I could make it happen, I excitedly said, "Well, I'm just getting back, but I'll find a way!" I asked her how

long I had to get out there, and she said 'bout a month. The only thing
was, Stan didn't want me to come into an office. He wanted to see me
perform live to see how the crowd would react to me, and I only had
four weeks to organize it all. *Damn, I need a show and a flight!*
I didn't know how I was go' pull it off. I just knew that I would!

The very next day I got a call from George Claiborne. He told me
that this cat named Bruce Jones, who I had met earlier on in LA with
George, wanted me to give him a call about an upcoming show he
was putting together. When I got on the horn with Bruce, he told me
that he wanted to book me for a show at this spot called the Knitting
Factory out in Hollywood. He told me that they didn't have a lot of
money, but they could fly me out, put me in a hotel, and put my name
on the flyers. I asked him when the show was, and he told me July 20,
which was in three weeks, right inside of my month window. Man!
This was too perfect! I couldn't believe it. I prayed for a way to LA,
with a show to go along with it, and God gave it to me.

As soon as I got off of the phone with Bruce to confirm the show,
I called Michelle and told her about it. She said she would invite Stan.

The time came for me to head back out to the Wild Wild West.
Long story short, after seeing a little of Hollywood, the show at the
Knitting Factory went great. I found it to be a very sexy, sultry spot.
It was a nice-size room, capable of seating a couple hundred people,
and it housed a great vibe. I ended up performing over a jazzy, hip-
hop flow for "Moon Cry" and brought the house down with "Wings."
I was on ten . . . thousand! I performed with so much precision and
energy that I surprised myself. I felt great.

After the show, Stan shook my hand, walked me over to a quieter
spot in the club, and told me that he really enjoyed my performance,
especially "Wings." He told me he loved the way I commanded the
crowd. Then he started telling me about "the show"—the tapings for
Def Poetry would be in New York, Mos Def would be hosting, and

it would be aired on HBO. I was thinking, *Damn, he's telling me an awful lot for me not to be on the show.*

But I wasn't a shoe-in yet. He asked me if I had a tape with me doing an a cappella version of "Wings." He said that he wanted to be fair and submit me to the talent committee, so I told him I could get him a tape the next week. While we talked, people kept kindly interrupting us to compliment me. I was feeling funny about the interruptions, but then again it was great that Stan could see how people responded to me. It was great standing there in this moment. It felt so surreal. A month earlier I was mad about missing my opportunity—now, here I was being invited to the show by the director himself.

After I made and submitted the requested tape, it was just a waiting game. I called and got great feedback from the *Def Poetry* people, I was feeling good, but the official word hadn't yet come down from the top. One day, after some weeks passed, I received a message from Bruce George, cofounder of *Def Poetry*. I immediately called back . . .

Ring

Ring

Ring

Bruce answered on the other side, and I said, "What up, Bruce?!"

"Who's this?" he asked.

"It's J. Ivy!"

"Ohhh, J. Ivy! I got something to tell you. Are you standing up or sitting down?!"

"Uh, I think I'm 'bout to sit down!"

Then he replied, "I just wanted to congratulate you. You've been selected to be on HBO's *Def Poetry*!"

"*Whattttt?!!!*"

I lost it! I screamed to the top of my lungs, dropped the phone, ran out the room, ran back into the room, jumped up and down, then picked up the phone out of breath saying, "My fault, man, my fault. This is like a dream come true!"

"Don't apologize," Bruce said. "Celebrate. You deserve it. You've worked hard for it!"

He told me that everyone loved my tape and that I was one of the best. He gave me some details about the show and told me if I didn't have a manager, I should get one, cause six million people would be watching. I told him that I was on it. He said that they would be in touch, and then I got off of the phone. "I did it! I did it!"

I said, "I," but "we" had done it. The guidance, belief, and ideas of my mother; the positive reinforcement of my brothers; the support, love, and inspiration of Tarrey; the help of Emmit and Michelle; the encouragement of my guys, my city, and everyone who ever put two hands together to cheer me on had propelled me to this moment.

The next few months were exciting—they had their ups and downs—but the anticipation of the upcoming show was fuel to keep me going. Individually and collectively Tarrey and I were rocking some cool shows, but at times we fell victim to the strain of inconsistent cash flow. I had to find a day job.

After an interview at a temp agency, I was hired as a sales rep for Dell Computers, which was a little crazy, 'cause I had never had a sales job before. I knew nothing about the field, but I didn't care. The money was good, and I was tired of struggling. I started on September 10, 2001, figuring that it would be temporary, with the high hopes of my career taking off after being on *Def Poetry*—especially seeing how *Def Comedy Jam* furthered the careers of comedians like Martin Lawrence, Chris Tucker, Chris Rock, Steve Harvey, Dave Chappelle, Mo'Nique, Cedric the Entertainer, D. L. Hughley, and Chi-town's own Bernie Mac.

And then 9/11 happened. The entire world was shaken by the crashing towers in New York City. It was a sad day in America, but it was especially sad for New Yorkers. Family and friends were lost on that day. Children were lost. Parents were lost. Brothers and sisters were lost. Coworkers and business associates were lost. City officials were lost. Policemen and firefighters were lost.

Like most people, I remember exactly where I was when terror struck. I remember watching the television at Dell's offices, thinking, *It's about to be WWIII*, and I'm sure a lot of other people felt the same way.

When terror strikes, the earth shakes,
And mourns the hurt that we've caused,
Without cause, we destroy one another,
Tear each other down,
Scatter fear across the landscape of our minds,
We're grounded by uncommon ground,
Disagreements,
Bereavement follows,
We're led by death,
The cold of the reaper's breath,
Our steps are haunted . . .
Hunted,
Our growth is stunted,
Stalled,
Our hope for heaven is hauled away,
With every innocent soul we slay,
We pray,
We forget,
Anger erases our memories,
Fury guides our ways,

We black out and become something we're not,
Filled with hate,
Love escapes,
And is lost to the hands of remorse,
The course of history is forever changed,
The beauty of our being is forever stained,
By terror . . .

The day after was the first day I didn't see a plane in the sky—not one single plane. The world was grounded. Fear filled the air, along with conspiracy and millions of evaporated tears. It was a very sad time. It's a very sad memory for America. To all the families, God bless you. To the fallen souls, may you rest in peace.

SHOWTIME ON HBO

The taping was moved to October 1 and 2, so I went to my temp job every day and waited impatiently for September 30 to roll around. When it did, I flew to New York. After 9/11 I was nervous about being on a plane, but we landed safely at LaGuardia Airport in Queens.

October 1, 2001, was one of the most amazing days of my life. Wanting to get a jump on things, I got up early, took a shower, ate, and then headed over to the Supper Club for the scheduled rehearsal time. The crew was all over the set, getting the cameras, lights, monitors, and sound together. Equipped with headsets, the production crew coordinated the next moves. A lot of talent was gathered there ready to rehearse, and then all of a sudden . . .

Russell Simmons walked in! Dammnnnn, the man himself! *It's official!* It was my first time seeing him in person. This was the real deal! This was one of those moments I'd been waiting for my entire life. I walked over to him, over to one of hip-hop's first moguls, humbly introduced myself to him, and sincerely thanked him for the opportunity. Russell, being cool and down to earth, thanked me as well.

Rehearsals started. I was nervous as hell with Russell sitting right there, but I did my thang. When I finished Russell said, "That was tight!" I thought, Dammmnnnn, Russell Simmons is feeling my work, but I kept my cool and calmly told him thanks.

There were two tapings each night, twelve poets on each set performing two poems each, and I was on the second set, so I had a little bit of time. I ate, got dressed, rehearsed in my room, then headed back to the stage area wanting to check out the first set to get a feel of how it would be. And believe me when I say the vibe hit me quick when I stepped into the once empty club, to now find it packed. The energy was crazy! And the folks who stood in the line that stretched the length of Forty-Seventh Street soon delivered more energy. There had to be a good eight hundred to nine hundred people there to see us poets rock the spot!

After the crowd was seated, Shang, a comedian and poet, came out and warmed the crowd up. He told joke after joke, getting everyone loose and ready for the show. I was watching on, leaning against the bar in the back of the club, when my longtime friend, comedian, and fellow Chicago entertainer B. Cole walked up.

"What's up, B.! Man, what you doing out here?!" I said, surprised to see him in New York.

He said he was headlining at Carolines comedy club on Broadway over the weekend, and Bruce, whom he happened to be cool with, had invited him over to check out the show. After giving me the rundown, he added, "Man, Coodie upstairs."

"For real!" I rushed upstairs.

"Chi-town up in here!" I said, excited that Coodie, another one of my guys from the Chi, was in the house. Not only was Coodie there, but so were my boy John Monopoly, aka John-John, and my girl Kelly, more Chicago friends!

I snuck up on John-John and said, "What up, fool!"

"*Ohh*, what's up, J. Ivy!" he turned around and said.

After we all said what up, John-John, asked, "J. Ivy, you on this?" referring to the show.

"Yeah!" I said. Man, everybody went crazy. I hadn't told a lot of people, and they were all hyped for me and the breaking news.

"You on the first or the second show?" John asked.

"I'm on the second."

"Oh, man! We're sitting in the front row, Chicago-style." He emphasized his words by repeatedly pounding his right fist into his left hand. We were all filled with an excitement, and the Chi-town pride was pouring out.

Right after that, Shang left the stage, and a voice streamed out of the overhead:

"From the planet of Brooklyn,
give it up for your host, Mos Def!"

Mos Def's mere presence charged the crowd. He made his way center stage as he pumped up the crowd, and then he hit everybody off with some jokes. He had everybody cracking up, and then he welcomed the eager crowd to the first taping of the first season of *Def Poetry*. He thanked them for coming out and taking part in history, and then he introduced the first poet.

One performance after the next, I watched in admiration. The poets were putting it down, so I knew I needed to get ready. I told my Chi-town peeps I'd see them later; they told me to represent, to do my thang, and that they would be sitting in the front row.

"4sho," I said and then dipped to my dressing room.

When I got to the rehearsal space, I put on a new orange Phat Farm turtleneck, courtesy of Mr. Simmons, and was back to rehearsing. The way the show was set up, each poet did two poems: a three-minute piece and a two-minute piece. Stan insisted that I do "Wings," so I figured I would take my time with that one. The only other piece that I had in my vault that fell under two minutes was "I Need to Write." I had never memorized it, so if I did it, I would have to read it from my writing pad. With no real time to adjust any of my other poems I decided to go with it. I pulled out my writing pad and started rehearsing.

I was super nervous, but it was now time for me to go to the set. I looked in the mirror and said to myself, "Let's do it, J.! It's your time," and then left the room.

When I got downstairs, I headed thru the crowded room and made my way backstage 'cause the first set was close to ending. Backstage, which was crowded with talent, I met the poets from my set, including poetic legend Amiri Baraka and the hilarious Dave Chappelle. I chitchatted a little bit with some of the folks but not for long 'cause my nerves were so bad.

While we were all sitting there, one of the stage directors came back to give us the performance order. Again, there were twelve poets per set, and for our set I was number eleven, with Amiri Baraka closing. By this time, the first set had ended, the second set's crowd had been seated; once again Shang warmed the crowd up, Mos Def kicked off the show, and the countdown began . . .

My girl Mayda del Valle kicked it off and snapped. My boy Poetri did the damn thang. Lemon Andersen rocked it. Dave Chappelle had everyone on the floor! And all of the other poets lit the stage on fire.

As each poet burst backstage after his or her performance, it was obvious the adrenaline continued to surge. Who wouldn't be pumped, having expressed on a stage of this magnitude? This was the biggest forum poetry had ever had in our age. It was every poet's dream for our voices to be heard and felt across the world. And here we were as the first, the pioneers. Here I was, one of a few dozen poets, selected from tens of thousands to be on a show, which was seen by millions around the world as opposed to thirty to forty people in a tiny coffee shop or a couple of hundred in a small club. This was our Olympics. And I had the pleasure of representing esteemed poets everywhere, my sweet city Chicago, and my family. This was it. This was history in the making. This was our big break. The wait was over. Finally it was my turn!

I had never been that nervous before in my life. I stood in the wings with my book in hand and my stomach in knots, waiting for Mos Def to call my name. And after a few jokes, he did.

*"Aight, y'all give it up for this brotha
from Chicago.
Put your hands together for J. Ivy."*

I walked out and was amazed by the size of the crowd. From watching the last set, I knew there were a lot of people, but the room looked so different from the stage. All I saw was a sea of eyes pointed directly at me. As I looked out at them, I walked toward Mos Def, gave him dap, and then walked to the center of the stage. Coodie, B. Cole, John-John, Kelly, and my girl Miche, who is also from Chicago, were all sitting to the left in the front row—Chicago-style! They cheered me on and represented so hard that it definitely made it easier for me, but as I opened my mouth and looked at all the cameras, I got more nervous.

Now, I should mention, my plan was to come out, pretend like I was so nervous that I forgot my poem, apologize to Stan and Russell, and then start pretending to write a poem, "I Need to Write," on the spot. The only problem was I had convinced myself that I really was nervous and became even more nervous. So nervous that I messed up the piece and had to start over.

Yes. It was the moment of my life, and I fumbled the rock, and the entire room stared at me in pity. I couldn't believe it, but there was no time to feel bad or be embarrassed. For a moment I looked like a rookie, but fortunately I recovered the ball, got on a roll, and warmed up, as I went on.

"Wings" was my money piece, so it wasn't a big deal that I was messing up the first joint. My mind told my mouth to rapidly rattle off the rest of "I Need to Write," just wanting to get thru it and on to my next piece. To my surprise, they loved it! Once I got thru it, the roar of the cheers made it obvious that they all felt it.

As soon as I finished my first piece, I refocused and went into "Wings." With a classic dose of J. Ivy precision, I killed it. No fumbles, no stumbles, just me smoothly revealing my soul. And when I finished, this very critical New York crowd stood up and gave me a standing ovation! I was in complete amazement! I went from a fumble to a winning touchdown, even though I was just getting warmed up. My adrenaline was pumping so hard that I wanted to keep rocking it, but I knew I had to leave the stage. I turned around to head off. B. Cole, who was standing up clapping, gave me a pound, and then it was over. The wait for my big moment went from years, to months, to weeks, to days, to hours, to minutes, to seconds, to history. It was over so fast. It was now in the past.

Before I knew it, I was back on a plane to Nashville, reflecting on the experience and what I had learned. I vowed not to ever allow nervousness to interrupt my dream and cheat me of the experience. I thought about the unnecessary stress I felt when I thought I missed my moment, and the power faith carries when you're willing to keep moving. I thought about the power of my gift. I thought about the love I received when I was comfortable and proud of being me.

Months later, when the show finally aired, to my surprise they showed me performing "I Need to Write" instead of "Wings." What hit me the most was how "I Need to Write," a poem that I wrote one morning out of frustration, was now being seen and heard by millions and becoming an anthem for poets all across the world. We do *need* to write, we do need to let go, we do need to dispose of the emotional weight that we carry, knowing that we will get to the destinations we desire.

Humbled to later receive a Peabody Award for my work on the first season, I was invited to perform on *Def Poetry* for two more seasons, 2005 and 2006. It just goes to show that when you follow your passion and trust your destiny, there can be so many beautiful and surprising sights along the way.

NEEDLE IN A HAYSTACK

With the success of *Def Poetry*, folks were now recognizing me wherever I went. I was beginning to receive invitations to perform in places I hadn't been. And people would approach me on the street and ask me if I was the guy who performed the poem "I Need to Write" on HBO. Overnight my popularity had grown. It was exciting to receive the positive feedback. It was great to see that so many people were inspired to write 'cause of something I madly wrote one morning in an attempt to relieve some stress. My vent became theirs, and it was motivating to be a voice for those who didn't have the courage or who didn't know how to speak up for themselves.

The success motivated me to keep moving. I wanted my message heard. I wanted to expand this journey of spreading healing and inspiration. I knew my options for that were either New York or Los Angeles, and after my experience performing and taping on Broadway for *Def Poetry*, I found myself bitten by the New York bug.

Some told me not to go to New York. They suggested I stay in Nashville or go back to Chicago, where people knew me. They told me that out in New York there were a million poets and that I would be a needle in a haystack.

Yeah, I thought, *but if you sit on that haystack, I bet you go' feel me.*

Why feel fear of living out your dream? Time goes by too fast for that. I always wanted to be the best. Not for selfish, egotistical reasons but to try and inspire someone, anyone who needed to be lifted the same way my words lifted me.

> *If you want to be the king of the jungle, you have to go to the jungle.*

You have to be willing to fearlessly fight for what it is you love to do. You have to have the courage to take those steps toward the war. Once you're in the fight, things flow from there, you defend yourself the best you can, you take the hits, you keep moving, you get knocked down, you get back up, you fight fair, you fight with heart, you fight for you and yours, you follow your instinct, you trust yourself, you choose your battles, and you fight to win. You have to know what you were put here to do and not let the traps of the jungle rob you of that joy. And it is joy. Exercising your purpose is your joy.

So that was the plan. Tarrey and I discussed it, and with her singing career on the rise, we felt a move would be a good fit for the both of us. Los Angeles was tempting, but New York seemed like the right first step. Before taking the leap, we decided to end our lease in Nashville, move back to Chicago for a few months, and stack some cash before heading out East. With the challenges our relationship had recently weathered, the plan for elevation had a few holes in it, but being each other's number one fan and supporter, we both wanted to see it thru. We agreed to work together, 'cause we knew what we had was true.

FEAR IS A HELL OF A DRUG

It was good to be back in the Chi hanging out with family and friends. The summers are always the best, with plenty of things going on. And being that I was the first African American out of the Chi to be on *Def Poetry*, everyday folk, the poetry scene, and the entertainment community were all showing me love. For the most part, I was in good spirits. I was looking forward to seeing where life would take me next. What adventure was waiting? I was encouraged, cruising on my high, intoxicated with the joy of living my dream. I felt there was nothing I couldn't do. There was no stage I couldn't get on. There was no mountain that I couldn't climb.

I was geared up and ready to keep things moving, but as the days and weeks went by, life became more and more stagnate. The rhythm that I was feeling was gone, and the daily grind was sobering. After feeling my independence in Nashville, after being out there and surviving the challenges of life, it was difficult adjusting to living at home again. It wouldn't have been so bad, especially with this being a planned pit stop, but the busyness of business that I left behind in Nashville hadn't followed me to Chicago. The goal was to stack cash for the move East, but nothing great was coming in. I had a show or two, but nothing was sustainable or savable. There was something so wrongly familiar about being back under my mother's roof, I felt I was not moving forward. I had been knocked off of my ladder, off of my mountaintop.

My stagnation became stressful. I needed to move. I needed to run and sprint. I needed progress. I wanted to hop from point *A* to *J* to *Z*. And then do it all over again.

I wanted and needed to keep growing, to stretch on and on like ivy vines grappling a ten-story building. Not moving was depressing. My flight had been grounded, buried in cement. I was back in the city where I buried my dad not so long ago. I was back to watching the days going by and feeling old losses and grief. Still not wanting to bring down Tarrey, my moms, or my boys with my weight, I felt like I didn't have anyone to lean on. Once again my pain and my downward thinking blinded my future.

Run, Forrest, RUNNN,
How does the terrain of the woods feel,
When you're exerting yourself like a mouse on its wheel?
I'm sprinting in place,
Moonwalking on Jheri Curl juice,
It's a slippery slope,
Let the chips fall where they may,
May I move?
Why do I need permission?
What happened to my rhythm?
I forgot how to dance,

I want to
Jack,
   Jack,
      Jack,
         Jack,
Jack my body,
But my mind won't move past go,
I'm jailed by overthinking,
The cuffs hurt my wrist,
My list of goals have been burned by the fires of doubt,
I pout tears,
Notes for my heart to hear,
Fear is a hell of a drug,
I'm tired of not singing about love,
Play my "Happy" song,
Pharrell where you at?
I want to get back to my happy place,
That space where I breathe easy during hard times,
I charge the wall of time without a helmet,
The box ain't velvet,
It's made of concrete, steel, and barbed wire,
In hell you don't do well bobbing fire,
Stick and move,
I'm waiting on the cool off,
The cool down,
Drive out, cruise, and find the cool in my town,
Trying to find the joy that I once found . . .

In that moment I forgot to be grateful for what I did have in my life. I forgot to live in gratitude. I was spoiled by the success I had been experiencing, and falling off of that high made me feel so low. Not doing led to no money. No money led to isolation. Isolation led me back to feeling depressed. *Depression led to not writing and doing what I naturally loved.*

With each step not being taken, I felt lower and lower. The negative spirits of old were haunting me again. Those negative voices were telling me that I wouldn't amount to anything, telling me that I would fail like my father did. Those voices were whispering to me that my dad left me 'cause I was worthless, 'cause I was nothing, 'cause I didn't deserve to be loved. Those same voices were telling me that the world would follow suit and abandon me.

Those voices were telling me to shut up,
to stop writing,
to stop performing,
they were telling me that no one wanted
to hear what I had to say.

Those voices told me that I was a fool. Those voices told me that I would never succeed. Those voices told me to give up. They told me that I was a joke. I was scared of walking down the hallways of manhood, fearful that I wouldn't amount to anything, fearful that the world, like my father, would leave me behind. I felt incomplete. I felt beat down. I felt defeated. I found myself in an ocean of discouragement and with each thought, I sank deeper and deeper! My confidence was gone. My world was turned upside down. I've never felt so down in my life. I felt like I was in hell!

I wasn't looking for it, but I had found my breaking point.

Swirling thru this habitual turmoil, I felt tortured by the unseen. I don't talk about this often, but one night I was spiritually attacked.

Early that morning, while the sun still rested, I woke up and saw something standing at the foot of my bed. Immediately I knew this dark shadow was some sort of evil spirit. Quietly it stood there. It had no eyes, but I could feel it staring at me. This easily could have been a nightmare, but I knew I was awake. I was wide awake. I knew I wasn't dreaming. Some may think I'm crazy or that maybe I was hallucinating, but I know what I saw was real. I laid there scared, frozen, not able to move, and screaming out for my mother, who was asleep in her room across the hall. I yelled at the top of my lungs, "Ma, Ma!!!" But my cry for help was muted by this thing that possessed me.

I listened to my hyperactive heart pounding thru my chest until I eventually fell back asleep, escaping my horror.

Later that morning I woke up confused, trying to make some kind of sense of what had happened. I wasn't able to fully comprehend what it was, but I'm a man with common sense. My instincts kicked in.

I prayed,
I prayed,
and I prayed some more.

I needed some spiritual protection from this uncommon energy. Lord knows I wanted whatever it was to go away. I was so drained and tired of the pain, tired of the negativity, tired of feeling crazy, tired of being sad, tired of the tears, tired of wasting precious time by not being happy and enjoying this short episode we call life. I was missing moments 'cause I was too busy suffering from old wounds. My spirit was being leeched on. I finally realized what I was fighting—my demons. And knowing what I was fighting, recognizing it, giving it a name allowed me to identify the problem and build a defense against it. I knew I could beat it.

I hear your doubts,
They pound in my head like a jackhammer chipping away at my
     concrete desires.
I hear your doubts,
They're deafening dousing the flames of my passion's fire.
I hear your doubts,
Sizzling like the acid you pour on my dreams.
I hear your doubts,
Your screams,
Taunting me,
Haunting me,
Confusing the instincts that drive me,
And my actions.
I've lost traction,
You tire me,
Trying to retire me,
Your doubts plaster their lies on me,
Trying to blind what my third eye knowingly sees,
Smearing the windows of my clarity,
My tongue begins to speak the hate you've planted,
The seeds you've slanted,
Slighted,
I hear your doubts,
Your commands,
My demons' demands,
My internal Klan,
Cloaked with white sheets,
And a cheat sheet of my weaknesses,
My demons and I grow so intimate,
Cozy,
You're so nosy,

DEAR FATHER

Noisy,
The chatter,
The clatter,
The clutter stutters my spirits' speech,
The ancestors preach,
So I reach back,
Listen with the intent to overcome,
Overhung,
Hung over,
Head ached by these drunken depressions,
But I got an Advil for the anvils,
Skills for the fears that seek and kill my will,
I will silence you,
Mute you,
Rebuke you demons.
Mama ain't raise no fool,
I know you're the devil's tool,
So I refuse to work with you,
I refuse to pledge an allegiance to you,
I have the power to decide,
My fate won't be compromised,
I won't sink in the sands that you've contrived,
Or give you the pleasure of finding joy in the tears I've cried.
I'll look ahead instead of looking back,
I'll hear your doubts fade to black as I change what I feel inside,
Silence your voice in this battle,
And survive . . .
Win . . .
Once again . . .
I'll come alive!

BREAKING THE CYCLE OF PAIN

It was now the first week of August 2002, and my disposition really hadn't changed. I was still in Chicago, confined to the walls of my old bedroom. In the midst of my nothingness, I managed to get a show. That one show sparked something in me. Something I hadn't felt since leaving Nashville . . .

Here I was, back on stage, after not touching a mic in months. It felt good to be back in my comfort zone. It felt great to be "home." It jolted me, woke me up. It recharged my spirit. It gave me a boost to start stretching out, but I knew that stretch needed to reach farther than the borders of my city. I knew it was time to go. Again I needed to clear my head of my familiar woes. I knew that meant getting out of the Chi.

The next week, I headed to New York for a visit. My mother didn't want to see me go, and Tarrey and I had a bad break up due to my isolation and terrible communication. In spite of all the thoughts that were swirling thru my mind, I touched down, and ended up staying. Within days I had an apartment in Brooklyn and work was already being thrown my way. I found myself flowing from studios to clubs, from commercial work to performances, always network-ing. It wasn't a real surprise that one thing led to the other, and my calendar swiftly filled up again. Before landing in NY, I had a feeling it would—I had faith that it would.

Even still, it's one thing to feel it, but it's another thing to see it come into fruition. I was there in this foreign town, standing as a man on my own two feet. I didn't have much money, but I did have an incredible crew of people that I kicked it with, and it felt great to know that I could take care of myself again, especially coming with nothing and starting over. Even without the security of a nine-to-five job, even when I didn't know where exactly my next check was going to come from, I believed that things were going to work out and doors were going to open. I was making it as a poet, as an artist. I was living the dream, my dream, and doing my best to ignore the pain of my recent nightmares.

The nightmares . . . I was out in the world exploring my fantasy, but I hadn't quite awakened from the dark spells that would continue to haunt me. The movement, the action of doing, would supply me with spells of amnesia, but like any drug, the effects would wear off and I would find myself hurting again in the halls of my mind. I desperately wanted to ignore the dark voices. I wanted them to go away, but they wouldn't. The voices of these terrible feelings wouldn't leave me alone.

"If you don't deal with your emotions, one day your emotions are going to deal with you." On one hand I was making a name for myself, but on the other I was feeling heavier and heavier. I couldn't shake the weight of the pain.

I couldn't stop thinking about my father.

The awakening I was feeling from the new environment and expe-riences was fading fast. My feelings were beginning to surface. I was mad at my dad all over again. I still stood on my forgiveness for him, but I was upset. Maybe I was still grieving. Maybe I was more filled with regret than I was anger, 'cause I only wished for the good things. I wished for the option of talking to him on the phone or going to see him. I wished I could let him know what I'd been up to. But I couldn't. In the midst of the successful commotion, I stood alone in the blind eye of the storm.

One night I was getting ready to hit the club when I got a call from my moms. As soon as I picked up the phone, I could hear the concern in her voice. All summer she had asked me what was wrong, but I constantly dodged the conversation. Now here she was, long-distance, asking me again. I felt like I was losing my mind, and her motherly alarm was sounding off. She knew that it was important for us to speak.

Maybe it was the timing of the call. Maybe deep down I knew she had the answers to my questions. Maybe I just needed to talk. I'm not sure, but for some reason I opened up.

My mask fell off. The tears fell as I somberly told her that I felt like a little boy who was afraid to become a man.

I told her I felt that I had been leaning on people my whole life, and I couldn't allow myself to do that anymore. I told her that I needed to know that I could be a man and stand on my own. I told her about what I saw at the foot of my bed months ago. I told her that I felt terrible for not being there for her and my brothers. I told her about what Tarrey and I had been going thru as a couple. I told her that I had a lot of questions about my dad, but mostly I was mad that he wasn't there.

That's when my moms *snapped*! For the next few minutes, she spoke to me with a Godly passion streaming thru her words. I could hear the tears in her voice, her pain. I could feel the truth being ushered from her spirit to my own. My mother has never been afraid to speak the truth. She's never been hesitant to speak her mind. Some call it tough love, but however you may label it, she's never sugarcoated her reality. It was what it was, so for the first time since my dad's passing, she opened up to me and spoke about him. After all, she was the one person who really knew and understood him. She shared a bond with him that no one else had: their marriage, their children, and their time together.

My sweet moms went on, reminding me to be grateful for the man my dad was. My mother had gone thru a lot with him, and she never spoke ill of him. She only remembered the good in him. I've always paid attention to that. So I intently listened to my mother's wisdom. Every syllable made perfect sense. Every bit of advice was carved out of perfection. She went on and on, the vibrations rising higher and higher, and then, with a thunderous tone carrying her command, my angel spoke as if the next message were delivered from the heavens,

Your father was a good man. Let him rest in peace...

Her words hit me like a bolt from God's rod, striking the core of my spirit. Something jolted inside. Immediately I could feel my life-long weight begin to melt. As always, my mother's words healed my soul. She was right. My father deserved to rest at ease. I needed to focus on the good in him and not the bad. So from that very moment, that's what I promised to do.

At the same time, my thoughts were swirling with things I had learned from my moms about my dad when he was younger. His parents, my grandparents, passed when my dad was young. He told my moms that when he was no more than four years old, his mother unexpectedly and suddenly passed away with him in her arms. He told my mother that they had to tear him from her grasp, as she held him tight even in death. It was rumored that she had been poisoned, murdered by his father's mistress. True or not, his mother was gone. After that my dad and his siblings were ushered around from one family's home to the next in their Southern Mississippi town, 'cause his own father had abandoned his children for his mistress. For years my dad was abused by his grandmother, and he escaped to Chicago as soon as he was old enough to leave. I imagined being him, young and hurt, without either one of his parents. I imagined him fighting thru the psychological and economical ailments that slavery left behind. I imagined the fear he must have felt, the uncertainty, and the lack of confidence. How could he trust anyone? How could he fully let go of his guard to love someone without fear of losing that person? My God! That must have been hard. It must have been a real struggle figuring out how to take care of himself, how to manage his feelings, his emotions, and his livelihood.

I didn't necessarily feel pity for him, but at this age I could empathize. I understood the struggle. I understood what it was to be an adult with real responsibilities. I understood how it was to have demons pecking away at your soul. I knew how it felt to lose your foundation. I wondered if my dad just never learned how to balance his feelings? Did he ignore them like I did? Did he figure everyone around him had it hard, and this was just how it was supposed to be? He had his passions working in radio and music, but was he disappointed with how the story unfolded? Did he feel bad for not reaching the top? I understood these kinds of questions.

I knew the battle was real. It was especially real 'cause he had his own children. He had young black men to nurture and raise. It was especially real 'cause his hurt—his own abandonments—followed and grew in him. The little boy inside of him never healed before he had little boys of his own. He never learned how to defeat his pain, find his happiness, so like anyone would have done, he unconsciously passed it on to me and my brothers.

His pain became our own. This was our inheritance . . .

For the next few days, the thoughts echoed on and on. The picture continued to grow. For the first time, I understood the full scope of my legacy. I grasped what it was to be a man who was always taught to bury his feelings. Society teaches us to do that. "Real men don't cry!" Real men hurt until their minds snap. Real men take their stress out on everyone they love. If that was the standard, then I was a real man. I was destroying the foundation of my future. I was making moves, but I was building it all on quicksand. I was on the run, but I was sprinting in place.

As I thought thru it all, I heard the voices of those who had shared encouraging words with me over the years. I heard my big cuz telling me to forgive. I heard words of advice, reminding me to let go of the past. I heard one of my college buddies telling me "pain is a temporary inconvenience." I heard my mother telling me her good memories of my dad. I heard Tarrey, who one day confronted me about my pain and challenged me to overcome it. She sweetly and simply said, *"You have to break the cycle."* *Break the cycle?! That's exactly what it was, a cycle.*

This pain was rewinding its revolutions, circling thru time, boomeranging past the boundaries of joy, and spinning one family after the other out of control. I was in fact on the wheel, circulating the same pain that was birthed generations ago.

My dad made mistakes, but he loved his family. He loved me. I wasn't abandoned. I was a victim of emotional circumstance. Generational curses, generational pain that had been passed down over and over and over again, to him, thru him, to me. Tarrey was right. This downward spiral had to end.

I needed to break the cycle.

Ever since my high school English teacher, Ms. Argue, "made" me do that live show, poetry has been my saving grace. I wrote "I Need to Write," 'cause the need is real. Poetry has helped me push past the pains of life. It's my prescription, my medication, my meditation, and my therapy. It's my release. With every poem I chip away at the strains life presents. It simply makes me feel better. Thru writing, I've learned a lot about myself. I've learned my strengths and my weaknesses. I've realized my value and my worth. I've realized that I have learned a lot by my father not being there. And 'cause of those self-teachings, my internal wisdom pushed my will to want for more. I didn't want to be a failure in life. I didn't want to let my mother and my family down. I didn't want my pain to drown out my destiny. I knew I had something special to offer to the world, and I didn't want my issues to block the history that could be made. I was put here for a reason, and I could no longer allow destructive emotions to stand in the way of my progress.

As I continued to reflect, I realized a lot of positive things about myself came from my father. My creativity, my ambition, my desire, and my dedication to my art—I had all learned from him, whether he actually taught them to me or not. My strong will, my sense of humor, my sense of style, my natural coolness are all him. My voice, my walk, my height, my beautiful brown skin are all him. I am a reflection of him. I am the next link in the chain of our legacy. Even though I self-ishly wanted more, my dad did his part. He got me here. There would be no me if there were no him.

I grew overwhelmingly grateful for the part he played. With my words aimed at the heavens, I sincerely thanked my dad from the center of my soul. Once again I forgave him. I forgave those people who had attacked me over the years. I forgave myself for the misery and stress I allowed to exist in my world. And with the strongest desire to move thru and past this pain that I had carried with me for years, like an untreated parasite, I decided to turn to my outlet, my medicine, and my therapy.

I needed to write!

Once and for all, I needed to put this pain down before it destroyed me. It was time. I was ready to be happy, so I picked up my favorite pen, I pulled out my trusty notepad, and with tears falling on to the blank page below, I began to write a poem, a letter, to my father.

DEAR FATHER

I wish you could have seen me do my thang,
I wish you could have been there the first time I sang,
I wish you could have seen how your baby boy flow,
I wish you could have seen me rock just one show . . .
Dear Dad,
These words are being written and spoken,
Because my heart and soul feel br o k e n.
I laugh to keep from crying,
But I still haven't healed,
After all of my years of my goofiness and joking.
You got me OPEN,
Hoping this ill feeling will pass,
Won't last.
I wear a mask so my peeps won't ask for the truth.
Truthfully speaking,
The truth hurts,
But I'm beyond hurting,
I'm in pain,

Why does it hurt so much?!
I find myself,
Fighting with myself every day to remain sane.
My peeps think I've changed,
Maybe trippin' off my fame,
But I'm still the same,
Still the same ole James.
I know it's a shame I don't come around as much,

But I don't want them to see me acting strange,
I don't want them to feel one
>   drop
>   of
>   my
>   rain,

But I can't seem to get these feelings to stop,
I can't get these thoughts off my brain.
Now when I really need to reach out for you, Dad,
And touch your hand,
I can't believe you're out of range.
I'm starving for your love and I'm begging PLEASE ease the crave.
When I was little,
I thought you left because I wouldn't behave.
Later on in life I found out that it was the cane,
As well as other thangs,
And with all the scars,
It was hard,
But I learned to forgive,
And forgave . . .
I forgave you for missing my basketball games,
And the touchdowns I scored at the football games.
I forgave you for coming home high and drunk,
Wrestling with my mother going insane.
I forgave you for missing all of my track meets,
And for not being there to greet all the pretty girls that I wanted you
    to meet.
I forgave you for missing my birthdays and graduations,
And not being there when I needed advice for certain situations.
I forgave you despite the fights,
The tears,

For all the years lost,
Wondering if I was loved.
Sometimes all I needed was a call and a hug.
I mean, I understand that people break up, don't make up,
And some relationships don't last forever,

But why weren't we together?!

Ma could have found a new man,
But where was I going to find a new dad?
Looking back,
I wished I would have begged, maybe pleaded my case,
'Cause I felt like I didn't matter,
Like I was deleted and erased.
I would cry,
And still cry so much that I get headaches.
I TRY TO GET YOU OFF OF MY MIND,
BUT I CAN'T GET YOU OFF OF MY FACE!!
I see you every time I see me,
And I can't do nothing,
But ask GOD to bless me,
Expand my territory,
Place HIS hands on me,
And to PLEASE keep evil far away from me.
I ask HIM to protect me,
Like I wanted you to protect me from the bullies and the police,
Now to protect my soul I write poetry and release.
And some say I'm a BEAST,
But I'm just trying to find peace,
So I can pick up the pieces of me that have fallen apart.
I've shopped all over for love,
And I've ended up with a lot of good items in my cart,

That helped me pull out the dart,

And helped me get out of the dark,

One being my art . . .

But along the way all of my decisions weren't so smart,

Because my love was amputated,

My life became complicated and my family . . .

Well Dad, I don't know if you knew or not,

But my sweet family became dysfunctional . . .

I remember,

I remember hiding under the dining room table when you and
   Ma would fight.

I remember dishes, pots, and pans being put in flight.

I remember the hole that you punched in the wall.

I remember when Ma called us from work and told us not to let
   you in,

And you broke in talking 'bout, "I'ma get y'all!"

I remember the alcohol and the smoke,

And going to the bathroom every five minutes so I wouldn't choke.

I remember you calling and telling me,

That I had a brother that died that I never knew.

I remember when you snatched my training wheels off of my little
   orange bike,

And making me ride when I was only two.

I remember when you pushed Ma and she broke her ankle.

I remember thinking,

"How could you do this to such a beautiful angel?!"

I remember Ma waking us up in the middle of the night saying,

"Shhh,

Jimmy,

Put some clothes in a Jewel's bag.

We're going to Grandma's . . .

And if your father come up to your school,
Don't tell him where we'll be!"
I remember spending Christmas at Grandma's,
Playing with my Stretch Armstrong,
Thinking, "Man, this ain't my house . . .
How did Santa Claus find me?"
I remember your stinky feet.
I remember all that pepper you would put on those ghetto meals,
That you would fix for us to eat.
I remember listening to you on the radio before I would go to school,
"WVON . . ."
I remember all those model cars and planes you would make,
And all the kids on the block thought that my dad was so cool.
I remember when you ran down the car,
And I was thinking,
"Damn, Dad's fast!"
I remember how you would curl your mustache,
    I remember the past.
        I remember the good and the bad.
            I remember thinking is this love false.
                I remember us moving to the burbs,
                and my boys replaced my love that
                was lost.
They would make me laugh and giggle,
And my boy even taught me how to dribble, so I could make the team,
And I did!
I thought that I would die without you,
But Rome, Todd, Dre, Ike, and Eric made sure that I lived,
And was never sad.
They even gave me their dads,
Mr. Kemp, Mr. Whitaker, Mr. Cross, and Mr. Price,

Became my dads,
My Cool Daddys!
But the little boy in me still wants his daddy, badly!
I feel like a scared little boy afraid to become a man,
But I think I'm ready!
I think it's time!!
I think it's time to shine and get mine!!!
I think it's time to shine and get mine,
So I can ease my mind and let my soul climb.

I think it's time to stand as a man on my
    own two,
Just like you used to do,
Before those demons started haunting you.
'Cause all I ever wanted to do was to make you and Ma proud,
And I wonder if you are,
I wonder if you know.
I wonder if you know that GOD gave me a gift.
I wonder if you know about the spirits that I lift.
I wonder if you know that I touch people with my words.
I wonder if you know that I inspire action with my verbs!
I wonder if you know that your baby boy did a show,
That aired for millions to see on HBO,
And that hard New York crowd that I didn't even know,
Actually gave me a standing O!!!
I know you know!
I know you're proud!!
'Cause I'ma be the best just like you wanted to be,
Watch and see!
And just in case you can't,
I'ma scream it so loud that I shake the clouds,

And move 'em out the way of my sunshine.
'Cause that's what you are, Dad . . .
James Ivy Richardson Sr.

Do you hear me?!!

You are my sunshine!

That's why I forgave you!
'Cause my love for you is still the same.
It may have gone thru a transformation,
But it never really changed.
So I swear,
On my mama and on my name,

I'ma stop this rain!
Conquer this pain!!
Make sure that you did not die in vain!!!

And when I get to heaven . . .
When I get to heaven,
I'ma jump in your arms,
We're going to kick back like when I was little,
And watch . . .
The Bears game!
I wish you could have seen me do my thang,
I wish you could have been there the first time I sang,
I wish, I wish that you didn't have to go,
I wish you could have seen me rock just one show!
I love you, Dad . . .

Live performance of Dear Father
http://tagr.com/t/V4cJRN

YOU CAN'T IMPRISON
FREEDOM

In that moment, I spilled my guts for my dad and the heavens to hear and take in. With the simple stroke of the pen, I let it go. My tears poured down and steered the ink on the page in new directions. It was the happiest poem I've ever written. It was the happiest I've ever felt. The weight that had been magnetized to my spirit had been lifted. The release of it made me appreciate everything I had been given. It made me a much better person. It made me a much better man. In that moment I knew that I could begin my life again. I could move forward without reservations, without guilt, without doubt or regret. I could rejoice in knowing who I am and where I come from. I could work on me with an honest heart. I could work on the parts about myself that I wanted to improve. I felt free.

I was free.
Free to move.
Free to truly be me.

Having broken thru the bars that held me for so long, I was now free to do what I was put here to do. Life is so short, too short to waste on depression and sadness. The pain had taken up precious space in my spirit, space that I would need in order to grow and become greater, greater for me but more important, greater for others. I wanted to be happy. I deserved to be happy. I needed to be happy. And now, somewhere within the strength of that moment, I had written myself a new lease on joy. I never felt better.

Shortly after writing "Dear Father," I decided it was time to share the piece with others. The easiest way to do that was by performing it at a show. Although the stage has always brought me comfort, when it came time to perform "Dear Father," it was more than a notion speaking my unguarded truth. The piece was so personal. It was so close to my heart. It was so close to my family, but those areas of vulnerability are where we find the depth of the healing that we're seeking. It was hard, but it was important to perform it where it all began, Sweet Home, Chicago.

In front of a packed house, my thoughts leaned on the comfort of my family and friends. It took every ounce of my soul to get the piece out, but what needed to be done . . . was done. Standing there with my eyes closed, I envisioned my dad, his smile. My spirit could feel his heart, which was warmed by the love that he had for me and my family. Supported by his spirit, my entire existence collapsed into the lines, letting the words catch me from my fall. Each word escaped my lungs with raw passion. My soul pushed out the purest poetic phrases with power and poise until the very last syllable. Like a track star, my energy was refueled by the love rediscovered, sprinting me thru until the last word dropped from my sincere lips. I was overwhelmed from letting go, but I felt empowered by the courage to speak. My strength stood tall, as a man's strength should, as I watched the audience rise, clap, cheer, support, and cry. We all became witnesses to the power of letting go, as I finally closed the door to my pain!

My pain was diminished. Each line had been medication, healing the wounds that had periodically reopened. My self-awareness became so much clearer. I acquired appreciation for both my good and my bad qualities, realizing that the imperfections had helped shape my character. Finally, I found love for the entire canvas.

I've always heard you can't love someone until you're able to love yourself, but before that moment it hadn't sunk all the way in. With love as my companion, it was my deepest desire to share my feelings, scream them from a mountaintop, make copies of these keys to freedom and pass them out for the world to hear. **Because of the POWER of forgiveness** I had broken the cycle.

I GET MY HYMNS FROM *HIM*

With this newfound freedom, my mind soared with renewed possibilities. My confidence grew tremendously. I valued my voice and my place. There wasn't a circle I couldn't stand in; there wasn't a poem I couldn't write. I felt free to create, develop my art, spread my wings, and shine brightly.

I found my cape, unmasked the victim inside, and became my own hero. I was a new man, and the timing couldn't have been more perfect. After all, I was back in New York. I needed to run faster than the pace set in front of me, so I prepared myself for anything that might come my way.

It
   was
      sink
         or
           swim.
So I swam.

I wrote.

I stroked the waves of my new moment.

With this preparation of the heart, my fresh outlook on life, and my success on *Def Poetry*, I continued knocking on doors. Always a lover of music, I found myself partnering with different musical artists in NY. I found it interesting how different music would bend my art and make me stretch in new directions. Often I would hear a musical track, and then I would hear a poem funneling thru my spirit. I loved the sensation—exploring and creating poetry with music, and collaborating with other talented artists inspired me to grow.

One artist in particular that I found myself hanging out with was this cat I met back home and was reintroduced to in NY. His name was Kanye West. Off jump, when I was invited to his New Jersey home, and he passionately performed for the seven or eight of us who were present, I knew that this guy was one of the special ones. His conviction, his dedication, his word play that he puzzled together over music that he produced was on another level. His work was something I had never heard before, but at the same time it felt familiar to my soul. His music was special, moving, and inspiring. He was the type of artist I wanted to work with; he was somebody who motivated me and positively challenged my creativity.

Kanye had built a name for himself as a producer for Alicia Keys, Ludacris, Jay-Z, and a host of Roc-A-Fella Records artists and was now shopping his own music around to different record labels. A lot of folks doubted him as an artist 'cause they wanted him to stay in what they thought was his lane. But Kanye wasn't going for it. He knew what he wanted for himself, and he refused to let others guide his heart. So he beat down the door of record label after record label, he made all the noise he could, until finally landing a deal with the label he had already produced a lot of records for, Roc-A-Fella.

I found myself in the midst of one of hip-hop's greatest climbs. Motivated by Kanye's movement and my own dreams, I beat the pavement and made my mark. While I was hitting different spots around NY, like the Bowery Poetry Club and the Nuyorican Poets Cafe, and branching out to colleges and universities around the country, one of my main buddies from home, Coodie, was making his mark in NY by directing documentaries and music videos.

Back in Chicago, I got cool with Coodie on the performance scene. While he always directed, being a comedian was also one of his earlier passions. Looking for any stage possible, I would hit the comedy clubs to perform my poetry, and I ended up getting cool with a lot of Chicago comedians, Coodie being one of them. Now living in NY with a camera in hand, Coodie was continuing his documentation of Kanye's journey after already filming him earlier on in the Chi. From the studio, to the concerts, to meetings, to Kanye's moves around the country, Coodie was capturing almost every moment.

Shortly after Kanye got his deal, he headed out to LA to record the rest of his debut album, *The College Dropout*. We caught wind of him getting into a near-death car accident. Everyone back East was shaken by the news, but we were happy to know that he was all right. It was evident that his destiny couldn't be stopped. The mission was real, and the music was needed.

One day I was driving thru Harlem with Coodie when Kanye called him up, even though his mouth was wired shut because of the accident. Coodie moved the phone from his mouth and said to me, "This dude ain't suppose' to be talking, and he's rapping!" As crazy as it sounded to hear that he was rapping through wires and unimaginable pain, it wasn't surprising. The man was determined . . .

Kanye told Coodie he needed him in LA, documenting what was happening. It was a life-changing moment, and he needed the world to see the process, so he flew Coodie out the following day.

Coodie called me up every day with exciting news from the West Coast. One day it was about the different folks who came thru the studio; the next day it was about hanging out at Jamie Foxx's house, where Jamie recorded his parts for Kanye's song "Slow Jamz." He would tell me about all the folks he was filming, how incredible LA was, and how I needed to get out that way. Motivated, I did the next best thing and started writing.

Saturday night rolled around, I wanted to hit the city to party, but I didn't have two dollars to even get on the train. I was in between shows, in between checks, but at the same time I was motivated and inspired. I thought to myself, *I got food. I got my pen and pad. I'm good.* I lit some candles, put on Common's new album, *Electric Circus*, and started writing. I've always known that I have angels watching over me, but the next moment was a great reminder of that.

It was now about eleven at night. I was sitting in my Brooklyn apartment, happy to be exercising my gift. With my notebook sprawled out in front of me on my bed, I decided to write the story about my dad and me miraculously reconnecting after so much time. I felt a sense of peace come over me as I was reminded of the beauty of our journey together as father and son. I was reminded of how powerful our prayers are. I was reminded about the strength and power buried in our forgiveness of ourselves and others. It felt therapeutic to be getting this story on to the page.

I caught a flow, and the words were pouring out of me, when I got a call from Coodie. I answered the phone with my typical "What it do," but Coodie was obviously excited about something.

"J.," he said, "you need to get to LA *right now!*"

Hearing the excitement in his voice, I said, "Why, what's up?"

"Kanye got a song with him and Jay-Z on it, and he wants to put a poet on it," he said, "and I told him he needs to put J. Ivy on it!"

Not believing the always funny former comedian, I laughed and said, "Come on, dawg, stop playing." It felt like one of those elbow-jabbing, "I got you" kind of moments.

"I'm for real, dawg!" he exclaimed. "You need to get to LA right now. Like, tomorrow, if you can. I told him you would be perfect for this song."

I said, "Well, man, if you're for real, I'ma find a way out there."

Being in the studio at the time, Coodie told me he wanted to play the song for me over the phone. I could tell he was making his way into another room 'cause the music in the background grew louder. I really couldn't hear the words on the song, so Coodie translated the distortion, telling me what Jay-Z was saying in his verse, singing along with the hook, and then telling me what Kanye was saying in his verse. After the song finished, he stressed his point again. He said, "J., get out here, man!"

Knowing the significance of the moment, knowing how big of an opportunity this was, especially with Jay-Z about to retire and Kanye about to take off, I told him again, "I'ma find a way."

I hung up the phone, and my first thought was *J., you need to write something right now.* I knew I had to figure out how to get to LA, but I didn't want to spend energy on finding a way and still have to write something when I touched down. I knew the moment was now. Action was what I needed to take, so I followed my instinct, turned to a blank page, wrote down the date, December 7, 2002, wrote down the title, "Never Let Me Down," and jotted down the first thing that came to my mind . . .

We're all here for a reason on a particular path,
You don't need a curriculum to know that you're a
part of the math . . .

After writing the first line, my mind went completely blank.

"NOOO!! NOT NOW!!!"

This wasn't the time for writer's block. This was my moment. I needed to write. I needed to put some words on the page. Not wanting to miss being a part of history, I started banging on the page while begging and yelling, "*God! I need a piece right now! Pleeaassee give me one right now!*"

After pouring out my soul to the Creator, I put my pen back to the page, and my hand started moving and writing, and writing, and writing, line after line after line. I didn't know what was coming out, but I knew not to stop the flow. I wrote till the page was filled, turned the page over, and wrote a few more lines. When I finished I turned the page back over, read the piece, and said, "Man, this is kind of hot!"

I couldn't believe it. I had just been stuck, and now the page was filled with this lyrical, poetic, spiritual mantra. I didn't know if folks would get it, but I loved it. With a big ole Kool-Aid smile on my face, I read over the piece about four or five times and called Coodie right back. I said, "Dawg, listen to this!"

Never Let Me Down

We're all here for a reason on a particular path,
You don't need a curriculum to know that you're a part of the math,
Cats think I'm delirious,
But I'm so damn serious,
That's why I expose my soul to the globe,
The world,
I'm trying to make it better for these little boys and girls,
I'm not just another individual,
My spirit is a part of this,
That's why I get spiritual,
But I get my hymns from HIM,
So it's not me,
It's HE that's lyrical,
I'm not a miracle,
I'm a heaven-sent instrument,
My rhythmatic regiment navigates melodic notes to your soul and
    your mental,
That's why I'm instrumental,
Vibrations is what I'm into,
Yeah, I need my loot by rent day,
But that ain't what gives me the heart of Kunta Kinte,
I'm trying to "give us-us free" like Cinqué.
I can't stop.
That's why I'm hot . . .
Determination, dedication, motivation,
I'm talking to you and my many inspirations,
When I say I can't let you or self down.
If I were on the highest cliff,
On the highest riff,
And you slipped off the side,

And clinched on to your life and my grip,
I would NEVER, EVER, LET YOU DOWN!!!
And when these words are found,
Let it be known that GOD's penmanship has been signed with a
    language called Love . . .
That's why my breath is felt by the deaf,
And why my words are heard and confined to the ears of the blind,
I too dream in color and in rhyme.
So I guess I'm one of a kind in a full house,
'Cause whenever I open my heart, my soul, or my mouth,
A touch of GOD rains out!!!"

When I finished the piece, Coodie lost it. He was screaming in the phone, "That's cold!! That's cold!! Hold on, J.!"

Moments later I could hear the loudness of the studio emerge in the background. I could hear a lot of people and music blaring thru the phone. All of a sudden the music turned down. The people went silent. Coodie's voice broke in.

"J.," he said, "I'ma put you on speaker phone. Spit that piece again."

Without hesitation I spit the piece like I had done it a million times. With perfection and every bit of passion in my soul, I sounded off this poem that spoke volumes from my heart. It was the epitome of what my spirit felt. Every word, every phrase cried out my pain, my joy, my willingness to overcome. It was God-given, and I wanted God to be felt thru my words. I wanted my voice to shiver the spirits of those listening. I wanted to touch them. I wanted to inspire them.

When I finished the piece, now for the second time, the room erupted with cheers. There was an explosion of claps and echoes of "Did you hear that?!" Everyone was so excited and me, well, I was by myself, broke, in Brooklyn, now standing next to my bed, looking around thinking, *Man, what's happening?! Somebody tell me some-*

238

thing! As soon as I had that thought, I heard Kanye say, "J., spit it again!" So I spit it again.

"Spit it again." I spit it again.

"Spit it again." I spit it again.

"Spit it again." I spit it again . . .

I spit that joint for a half hour, and the piece is only a minute long. Coodie finally got back on the phone and said, "J., guess what." I said, "What?" He said, "Kanye's flying you out here tomorrow." Wow . . . I found my way!!

One minute I was alone, writing my story, knowing that my work would continue to touch the world. The next minute I was calling my moms, waking her out of her sleep, reading her the new poem, telling her this life-changing story, and borrowing a few bucks before my upcoming flight out West. When I read her the poem and my bluntly honest moms told me she loved it, I knew I was ready to get on the plane. I was ready to head out and get on a record with Kanye West and Jay-Z.

To this day I get chills just thinking about the magic of that moment. There I was, doing what my instinct told me to do, which was to write, and an incredible opportunity knocked on my door, and because I was spiritually ready to receive it, because I was open, because I was at ease, because I was relaxed, because I was confident, because I was free, free of my stress and my pain, because I hadn't let fear and doubt get in the way of being in this position, because I trusted myself, because I took my leaps of faith, because I dedicated myself to what I love to do, because my passion wouldn't allow me to get in the way of my movement, because I believed in myself and my ability to channel God's word, because I was able to forgive my father, remove the pain that was taking up so much space in my life, and replace it with a loving power,

I was able to deliver. I was prepared for this blessing. I was prepared to "get my hymns from HIM."

People have sent me pictures with my verse tattooed on their arms. People have told me my verse helped them thru school, thru break-ups, and thru rough times. People have told me that they start their day by listening to it. When they're down or depressed, they play it. Folks have told me that they work out to it. Teachers have told me they teach it to their students. Students have sent me videos of them performing it. Music lovers tell me that it's the greatest verse ever performed in hip-hop. I've heard someone say they want it to be played when they're lowered into their tomb. Several people have told me that when they were at their lowest point, their breaking point, this poem, this piece that I humbly prayed to God for, prevented them from taking their own lives.

This poem has given countless people hope, including me. When I'm down, when I need a reminder of the possibilities, when I need a boost of energy, this poem and the reactions of others have lifted me up. This poem has kept me going in the hardest of times. It has been my inextinguishable light. We all have that light in us. We all have seen or done things in life that are unmovable placeholders for the beauty we are capable of producing. Most times we just have to remember who we are. We just have to remember where we come from. We have to remember where we are going.

February 10, 2014, marked the ten-year anniversary of Kanye West's debut album, *The College Dropout*. It's amazing to see how fast time flies, but when *Billboard Magazine*, *Complex Magazine*, and Revolt TV contacted me for interviews, it was more amazing to realize I was a part of a project that could stand the test of time. The creative process for this album had been electric, to say the least. The entire experience was magical. Everyone who was involved knew that it would be an album that would make waves, that it would be a tsunami changing the course of how music is created, received, and appreciated. Because of the stories told, the lyrical word play presented, and the majesty of the soulful production poured out, because of the guest musicians and artists who put their hearts and souls, the overall vision of this work of art, and the persona and genius that is Kanye West, *The College Dropout* went triple platinum, won a Grammy, and was deemed by many as the album of the decade and one of the top hip-hop albums ever. It forever changed the music game. And because I had the strength to let go, because I was prepared, I will forever and always be a part of the history that was made.

From *The College Dropout* to my own albums, "Here I Am," "Diggin' in the Papes," and "LIFE after Life," I've always looked to translate my spirit's language thru music as well as poetry. Whether I'm collaborating with hip-hop, soul, country, alternative, rock, or blues artists or creating projects of my own, I look to find that energy that will speak to our universal souls and remind us that we are all connected, we are all one. That is where I find joy. In the simple task of breaking down worlds of misconceptions and misdirection that guide us further apart. The job of my poetry and my music is to bring us closer together and to remind us of the beauty, light, and love that we all already possess.

Prepare for the opportunities coming your way,
Get out of your way,
Don't think.
Let your instincts drive you,
Guide you down the road,
There is so much love inside of you waiting to be introduced to the
    world,

Let it speak and shake hands with mankind,
Let your love find the kindness in every woman and man,
Showing them keys of compassion that they can instill in their children,
Activate and start rebuilding what the old you destroyed.
Employ to be better,
Sever ties with the lies that stumble your walk,
Know you can,
Know your worth,
Your value,
Don't let others price check what's priceless,
Trust yourself,
There's so much left,
The mission is far from over,
Lighten the weight on your shoulders,
Push with purpose,
Snatch the fear out of your spine,
When your stars align be ready to shine,
Don't ever give in,
Or blend in,
Stand out,
Stand proud,
Write your story with your soul's pen,
And then . . .

IT TAKES A VILLAGE

It was three in the afternoon, and I walked into the small library of a Chicago public school on the South Side. With bookcases and books—along with celebrity posters encouraging students to read—flanking us, Tarrey and I prepared to facilitate an afterschool poetry and songwriting workshop. I was eager to share my knowledge with the next generation of poets, writers, and leaders, grateful for being invited out by the principal.

After pulling out a stack of new gold and maroon journals, gifts from Deepak Chopra and the Chopra Foundation for the students, I stepped to the dry erase board and wrote *I Need to Write*, in big, bold letters with a black marker. Seventeen students filed into the library, excited and ready to write. Ranging from first graders thru eighth graders, they talked and joked until Tarrey and I got their full attention.

To begin, we let them know how excited we were to see them there, we let them know how much fun we would have exploring the stories of our realities and imagination, and we went over some goals, objectives, and expectations for the sessions.

I wanted to show them how my story might relate to their own, so I asked them to raise their hands if they were living without their dads at home. Out of the seventeen students, one's hand stayed glued to the desk. I wasn't surprised, but it still does something hurtful to your spirit to know that these young, bright, intelligent beings were missing out on the guidance of their fathers, and their fathers were missing out on experiencing the beauty of their children's growth. I still don't understand the complete absence that takes place. How does one abandon this special piece of shelf?

Wanting to break down their emotional walls and spark their courage to write their own stories, I performed "Dear Father," then told them, "If you don't deal with your emotions, one day your emotions are going to deal with you." Quickly they turned to their new journals, picked up their pens, and got into their zones. Their instincts took over, their creativity kicked in, and they wrote line after line. Once everyone was done, they were excited to share their poems.

My first reaction was that these young folks could really write, but that was followed by an overshadowing discomfort I felt once I was able to absorb the content of their work. They were honest. They were hurting. Their confidence was waning. They lacked hope. They understandably had no trust in their absent fathers.

Seeing those kids' reactions to "Dear Father" was beyond inspiring. The story I'm telling, the story that I've prevailed thru, is a real-life story so many others also live. I pour out my heart, and they reflect on theirs, but when the class ends, many of these young folks who do not receive full-time love from their fathers return to lonely and challenging homes.

Our children—I say *ours* because it does take a village to raise a child—are hurting. Many of them live in single-parented homes. Many of them are struggling in impoverished environments. Many of them feel cheated. Many of them are being slighted.

And then they take the blame for their parents' choices, for society's ills. Their esteem is shattered. They become battered by the insecurity that sways every decision they try to make. They feel less of themselves. The enthusiasm to learn and better themselves is destroyed because they don't see their value. Their confidence is cut in half, and the brutal honesty of other children further complicates their view of themselves. It's a lonely place to live in. Bullies bully 'cause they are lonely, hurt, and afraid. The bullied don't speak up, 'cause they are lonely, hurt, and afraid. The vicious cycles are exchanged. Victims victimize one another. Compassion hasn't been learned because no one at home has had compassion for them and their well-being.

A mother without a present partner has only so much time. She has to work, struggle, fight to take care of her children, so the nurturing she would naturally give is given to the nine-to-five, given to the graveyard shift, given to keeping a roof over their heads and food on their table. The hole digs deeper. The fall feels endless. The gap is widened. The bridge to learning how to properly treat one another has long been burned down and forgotten. The ashes become the pollution we choke on. Our futures become asthmatic.

When I stood in that classroom of some of the brightest young people I'd ever met, it was obvious to me that their minds had the power to move mountains. Their insight on topics, their outlook on life was beyond their years. And their eagerness to learn, their eagerness to shape their insight was inspiring, to say the least. They wanted to speak. They wanted to express themselves. After breaking the ice, they desperately wanted to voice what they felt. It was obvious they just needed the chance, and now that they had it, they jumped at it and didn't let go. When I asked them to write, they exquisitely wrote with a passionate fury. Electricity ran thru them, and it was clearly heard when they read the lightning that had struck the page.

Be it positive or negative, children are honest. Their thoughts spill out thru their conversation. They aren't as guarded as adults. Yes, there are the quiet ones; yes, some don't want to write. But when they speak, it's real; it's whatever is in their heart. Some of them express it thru anger. Some of them express the fact that they don't trust their father because of the absence. But this day one young girl really struck a nerve when she said in her poem that she felt worthless.

To hear this young beacon of light say that she felt worthless was heartbreaking. This gifted child couldn't see her light because it was shaded by her pain. She didn't realize how intelligent she was. She didn't realize how creative she was, and because of that she couldn't see her future. She couldn't see the possibilities before her. She couldn't imagine becoming the dreams that she dreamed. She couldn't see her power to touch and inspire others. None of the students could.

But thru conversation, writing exercises, and a series of performances, the pain was breaking down. Each piece the students were able to write exposed their lights. They were beginning to see themselves. They were beginning to appreciate themselves. And that same child who once felt worthless quickly changed her thinking. With each poem that filled her notebook, she could see the greatness that she possessed. Each child found a pride that had been missing. The students established trust in themselves, even if they couldn't find it elsewhere. Revealing what was already inside, they discovered themselves and their value, which showed me how important it is to get this message out there. This was one class in one school, a microcosm of what the world is currently facing.

It is our duty to help our children see their light. We all have to do our part. We need to make sure our children are staying out of trouble. We need to keep our eyes open, protect, and nurture. The world isn't the big ball of peace I wish it was, but we can start making a difference by talking to our children. We can take a few minutes to give them advice. We can be quiet and listen to the intelligence and insight of our young future. Our children need us, and we need them. Our babies should never feel worthless when they are worth so much. It is critical that we come together as a community, lift one another, because we are, in fact, one.

Each one . . . teach one.

DADDY LOVES YOU

The morning of September 10, 2013, I streamed slowly out of a dream. I had slept only three hours that night, but I slept hard. I stayed for a while in that space between the dream world and the real one, but the visions I received from my dream were so vivid and clear.

For the first time in a long time, I saw myself with my dad. We were in a lounge, a small lounge, one of those 1970s-vibe lounges. The ones with big orange and brown pillows circling the floor. Maybe it was a recording studio? I'm not sure, but the place was home to a very hip crowd. As I looked around, I realized that my dad and I were working together! We were the hosts of a party, and it had all the elements of a funky good time. Fifteen to twenty people were talking, laughing, mingling, and soulful background music carried the mood. The music was so hypnotic. Everyone was grooving, taking it all in. Everyone was feeling it; everyone was having a great time.

The record was coming to an end, and my dad headed to the booth that sat off to the side. *Wow*, Jim Richards was back on the mic. Years after his death in the real world, my dad was still living his dream in the dream world.

As my dad exited one way, I headed into another side room. I could hear my dad over the speakers stopping the record and making an announcement. My father's voice was golden. His words vibrated the room like *giants* wrestling in the clouds. Like a bass guitar, it could be felt in your core, strumming the strings of your soul. It was strong. It was peaceful. It was calming. It was soothing. It was magical. It was hypnotic. It was therapeutic. It was engaging. It was warm. It was angelic.

Guiding the small crowd of people thru the inspiring ride we were on, my dad said, "I have a song I want to sing." He sounded amazing. The man was *sangin*! More than his voice, the words and the melody struck me. Each lyric was perfectly written, perfectly spoken. The melody cruised thru my spirit, as these words spoke directly to me. He was singing to me!

"Daddy, Daddy loves you,
Ooooo, yes,
I love you,
Ooooo, ooooo . . .

Immaculate conception,
Hmmm, mmm, mmm,
Immaculate affection,
Hmmmm, mmmm, mmmm,
I can't see you,
Not being in my life,

I can't see this world,
Without my Wife,
Hmmm,

Daddy really loves you,
Ooooo . . . oo, yes,
I love you,
Ooooo . . . oo,
Daddy really loves you,
Ooooo . . . oo,
Daddy really loves you,
Ooooo . . . oo . . ."

Hearing the song, I raced back into the main lounge. Not surprised by the expressions of admiration that were now dominant in the room, I noticed a guy filming the people's reactions on his phone.

Immediately I asked him, "Yo, did you record that?"

"Yeah," he said.

Filled with a new sense of pride, I excitedly said, "You know that's my dad, right?"

"Yeah," he said, "I recorded it for you . . ."

As he said the word *recorded*, something triggered inside of me, prompting me to act fast, so I reached for my iPhone in the real, waking world. I pulled up my voice memo and hit record. I couldn't pull all of my dad's words thru to this side. They were lost in the space between dream and reality, but the essence of the song was in my soul.

I woke up fully with my face drenched in tears of joy; I was in a peaceful shock over what I had just witnessed. I absorbed the moment, I reflected on it, I lived in it, knowing that my dad watches over and protects me, my brothers, my mother, my wife, his sister . . . my family. I lay there knowing that my dad is with me every step of the way.

I know he gets to see how his baby boy flows! I know he gets to watch me rock every show.

I know I have angels that have been assigned to be my guides. In an instant, I realized that hindsight is twenty-twenty, but faith is blind.

Fully awake and overwhelmed with joy, I heard the following words . . .

After fighting thru the echoes of endless screams,
Last night,
My daddy sang me a song,
In my dreams . . .
Dad, I love you too!!

The peace I felt in that moment softened every ounce of hardship I had ever experienced over the years. I came to realize that every single event, joy, pain, story, lesson, blessing, curse, struggle, and reconciliation is all tied together to help paint the picture our spirits need displayed in order to see who we really are. Our vision boards fill up over the years, guiding us to the next chapters. We become more complete. We bridge the gaps of our understanding. We begin to effortlessly wade in the waters of our purpose. "We are all here for a reason on a particular path," and the reason becomes more evident. Our clarity becomes more precise. Our value of time and what we do with it becomes more obvious.

Our gifts become our weapons to combat the emotions we war with.

Our gifts become our peace to create our art with.

My art allowed me to create. It allowed me to find my peace. It allowed me to look within, to look in the mirror, to forgive, and ultimately to reconnect with my father. It allowed me to see that the weaknesses of his humanity became my superhuman strength. My dad is my superhero. I can see that now because the Smoke has Cleared, my Dreams are no longer Fractured, Broken Up, or Broken In. My Little Boy Blues became this grown man's favorite song. My Birthday Wishes have come true. My Home has grown Sweet again. My life's training wheels have been snatched off, with my dad, once again, pushing me out into the world, knowing that I would find my balance on my Search For Freedom. In this moment we became closer than ever. And I feel calm knowing that the closure I was able to find allowed us both to open new doors. Our souls are no longer tortured. I am no longer haunted by my fears. And I believe that my father feels the same. I believe that he is now able to truly rest . . . in peace.

FINDING YOUR VOICE

I hear voices. No, I'm not crazy. At least not all of the time, but I do hear spirits. I counsel with this committee, their voices reverberating in the inner chambers of my soul. They are my spiritual friends, my voices of reason, a vocal troop that translates my body language, guides my steps, and paves my path. Think of them as a colorful painting on the walls of my imagination: blue hope, green growth, yellow fears, red rage, orange light, black holes, white noise, violet victories, speckles of spectrums that ignite the engines of my colorful curiosity, creating, curating, and carving out the change that occurs in my consciousness.

How do you manage the voices in your head? How do you manage the committee? How do you manage your board of directors that direct your direction? Rarely do they whisper. They're proud, so they speak with no remorse. They have no restrictions. They hold nothing back. Without my permission, they speak . . . freely. They own the floor. They built it. They wax it. They slide on it in white tube socks laughing at their control over me. You see, filters don't dwell here. They keep it real.

But what you don't feed will die. Your attention is the light that energizes their growth. Let your conscience be your guide. But the guru that is *you* becomes true when you recognize their presence, discipline your control, conduct your train of thought as you guide your conscience. These voices, these messengers that fight to deliver what they feel is right, are not always right and not always wrong, and it is up to you to listen, distinguish, silence, or empower the different members of your committee—the cast of your consciousness. It is up to you to cultivate the garden that is your mind, weed out the diseased thoughts, and water the truths of your present moment.

The Committee

Doubt

Don't do that! It's just not a good idea. No one cares. Those friends, your family, those folks who told you not to go that route, were right. Stop wasting your time. Let it go.

This voice is the complete pessimist. Doubt is always negative. With fear as its heart, Doubt is void of faith and doesn't have belief. Listening to Doubt, you always feel like something is going to fail. The bridge to your goals will crash, burn, and crumble with you on it, Doubt says, so you are discouraged from trusting the moment, yourself, or others. Thriving on low self-esteem and a lack of confidence, you are constantly reminded that you are not good enough, you are not equipped with the skill set to succeed in the moment or the moments to come. Doubt uses flashes of past setbacks as its calling card.

Passion

You love this! This is what you were born to do! Come on . . . let's show the world what you are made of . . . and shine!

Passion is the burning fire of your soul. Passion is the coal in the furnace of your purpose. Passion is the voice that pushes you to chase your dreams and the voice created alongside of your destiny. It knows exactly why you are here and encourages you to become that. Passion has no doubt about who you are and who you will become. Passion sees the future; it pulsates in the heart of your deepest desires. It doesn't settle for less but is pained when you do. It doesn't understand when its voice gets lost in the shuffle but never tires of screaming your soul's mission statement.

Clarity

Remember who you are. Remember why you are. Visualize where you want to be. Take a deeeppp breath. Feel the smile of your heart. Feel the texture of your dreams. Relax your muscles. Calm your mind. Walk in the footsteps of your desires. Breathe.

Clarity is the voice of your peace and serenity. Clarity is your calm in the storm of noise. Clarity relaxes and soothes you; it allows you to see your Passion. Clarity is the space between each breath rejuvenating your mind when it grows tired; this is where epiphanies are found. It's your perfect horizon. Clarity is your perfectly blue ocean. Clarity is the perfect sunset, the perfect sunrise, the tropical breeze cleansing your thoughts of chaotic-ness and clutter. Clarity is easy and positive, and it always makes sense because Clarity is the foundation of your true self. It is your meditated soul, and it is the wisdom found behind closed eyes.

Envy

Man, that's wack! I can do that with my eyes closed. Who gave them this opportunity? They think they're all that . . . wait till I get my chance to shine. I'll show them how it's supposed to be done.

Envy drives the demon's psychology and actions, and its only job is to contaminate your mind. Envy can never be happy for others, so it convinces you to downplay the accomplishments and desires of family, friends, and others. Envy and jealousy go hand in hand, and the objective is to knock everyone down in order for you to feel better, stronger, and more talented. Envy squeezes out your ability to love and blinds you to reality. It doesn't allow you to find appreciation in the beauty we all create or the chance to collaborate; instead Envy isolates you in a dark corner.

Creativity

You got a story to tell, so tell it. Put it on display. Your imagination was meant to be seen, meant to be felt. Feed your passion. Don't cheat the world by not giving people the beauty of your gifts. Inspire them!

This voice is the therapist. It's the release, the outlet, for all the others. It is the mirror for every other thought, opinion, and fact. It's the battery of imagination. Creativity builds new worlds to replace the ones destroyed by the past. Creativity is joy and fun; it tickles the spirit and surprises you with its countless creations. Creativity is the bridge of dreams and reality, and it is Passion's sweet sword slicing thru the voids of life. It's your inner child's favorite playground. Creativity paints your future with peaceful strokes of genius and fills your soul.

Confidence

Remember who you are. Your visions are validated by the love you feel for them. Speak with assurance. Tackle your goals and drive thru. Your worth can't be measured.

Confidence is being proud of who you are. With its chest out and head held high, Confidence glides into any room, knowing you are a star, a light for the world to see. Confidence believes in you and your ability; it hears the roars of Passion and Creativity. It thoroughly believes in them and because of that, it is Doubt's arch nemesis. It is the voice that promotes the good in you, your higher self. It is aware of your potential, aware of the gifts that have been given, and with pride works hard at reminding you and the world of your greatness.

Instinct

Think fast! Your intention will shine thru. Get out of your way. Trust yourself. Move!

This voice doesn't have time to think. Triggers are pulled, and it fires. It kicks upon contact. It's the truest definition of cause and effect. When things come around, without thought Instinct comes right back around, responding with a quick force. Instinct is that gut feeling, intuition, your third eye. It's your sixth sense, your Spidey sense. It's that churn in your stomach when something is wrong. Most of the time, Instinct is right. It's your direct connection to the Guardians and the Creator, who give you a supernatural guidance that always supports you.

Overthinker

My gut is telling me to do that, but what if it doesn't work? If I make that move, what is my next move? What will people think if I do that? How will I explain myself? What if?

Everything is analyzed—the Overthinker questions and second-third-fourth-guesses most situations. It often dwells in the past, replaying past situations in a constant loop, trying either to make sense or to fix what occurred. It confers with the other voices—Confidence, Doubt, Creativity, and the Judge and the Juror—but it has a beef with Instinct because Instinct doesn't give the Overthinker a chance to shine; like oil and water, they don't mix. The Overthinker's problem is not having self-trust and not taking action.

The Judge and the Juror

Why did you do that? What were you thinking? I can't believe you fell for the temptations. You're weak for doing that. And looking at your track record, you're more than likely going to do it again.

The Judge and the Juror are cold and malicious. They cut you down and criminalize you for the decisions you've made. They are merciless and unforgiving; they don't allow you to grow, but instead the Judge and the Juror condemn and punish you for making the mistakes in the first place. They instill the fear of Doubt so that you are too timid to take any risks that might help Passion, Confidence, or Creativity.

The Demons

No one is good enough for you. They don't love you. You're no good for anyone anyway. You might as well give up! No one cares what you do or that you exist. We hate *you!*

The Demons . . . the Demons are the gateway voices to your dark side. They are the persuaders and the tempters. They are the "Awww, come on try it!" voices that place the carrot on the string being reeled along by the master they serve. They are the snakes in the garden, the trap in the woods, that creepy creaking of the attic floor. They strike your insecurities, your triggers, and the weaknesses of your mind. These voices ignore the Creator's warnings, and they don't take heed of the mistakes from the past. They are lurking in the shadows, working hard at conquering your spirit, stealing your soul—the generals of your negative foot soldiers; they are the captains of your fear. They are only silenced when we have the discipline to do right, when we have the discipline to operate in complete compassion and love.

The Guardians

We have been sent here to protect you, to help guide you. We will open doors for you and give signs for you to follow. We are always with you, so you're never alone. Slow down, breathe, and listen for our word. We love *you!*

The Guardians are one with the Creator and the higher spirit of your human self. The Guardians are the sweet angels that you have been assigned to, or that you have chosen. They are links in your chain back to the Creator, and like your connection to your parents, you are deeply connected to the Guardians. The Guardians don't always speak, but they make sure to make their presence felt. They are the ancestors; they are the links to your past and your future, the before-life and the hereafter. The Guardians are kind, gentle, and wise. The Guardians are loving and peaceful and protect you from the Demons—when you don't ignore their help.

The Creator

You were created in my image. Your gifts have been wisely chosen and are unique to you and you alone. Walk with faith and the warmth of my guiding hand. Remember to show compassion. Remember to share what you have learned. Empty your plate so I and I alone can refill it. Remember to bathe in the glory of my light and my love.

God, Great Spirit, Allah, Messiah, Buddha, Universe . . . the Creator speaks thru sound, color, feeling, taste, music, poetry, stories, a churning of your stomach, and the raise of the hairs on your arms and neck. That guidance is heard thru Instinct, our thoughts, and our love. The Creator is the purest, most beautiful form of unconditional Love. The Creator created every single facet of our universe, our existence, and you hear it in your dreams, your prayers, and your meditations. You hear the Creator's voice when you create, when you meditate, when you dance, when you slow down and breathe deep. The Creator is omnificent, and because of that you are surrounded by its Love. You hear its guiding voice, that voice that encourages you to be every single thing the Creator created you to be. The Creator is Peace. The Creator is the happiness found in our gratitude. The Creator is Love, a beautiful light shining bright in your spirit, urging you to find your voice . . .

Your Voice

Your voice is a disciplined combination of all your voices . . .

It's the master of these students romping thru the classes of our lives.

Teacher, teacher,

Your voice is alive,

It has power that you haven't even tapped in to,

It's true,

Every voice is in you,

Softly whispering to the navigator of your spirit,

You hear it,

Clearly,

Steering your thoughts,

Who will you listen to?

When these voices fight to be heard what will you do?

Every emotion exists inside of us.

We choose which ones to empower.

Who do you give your power?

Hour by hour I'm driven by Passion,

My Instinct and Clarity yearn for me to be fearless,

I try to ignore the Envy in me,

But the Doubt ties my feet,

My spirit goes unfed,

When the Judge and Juror hang the past over my head,

When I'm free and Creative they say I'm over my head,

I'm out in space creating new worlds,

Confident,

Floating on a dreamer's dime,

But at times the Overthinker in me grounds me,

Fear surrounds me,

Meets me at the crossroads of my decisions,

Tells me that I'm too old to go down roads like that,

I'm too young to do this and that . . .
When those thoughts become my truth,
The truth hurts,
So I wear my mask,
I hide my hand,
My growth is stunted,
These voices scream at me,
I feel their tones in my bones,
Vibrating the concrete I stand on,
I stand alone with my committee of voices,
Echoes of choices that choose my destiny,
Urges that urge me,
Nudge me in different directions,
These voices infect me with their affection,
I agree and go along with it,
My conscious goes along for the ride,
My tour guides,
My voices,
They try to steer me with their ideology,
Without an apology or remorse for the discourse,
This course is decorated with the designs of my interior,
My core speaks and reigns superior,
Guilty pleasures,
Hidden treasures are buried there behind my eardrums,
Beating my brain with the rhythm of their ways,
Their sound waves in the stadium of my mind,
These voices are daring,
Deafening,
Blaring,
Doctors say I'm schizo,
There goes my vertigo,

DEAR FATHER

Off balance is my challenge,
I try to mute the Demons that my Guardians rebuke,
Let go and let GOD guide the echoes of my dreams,
I hear echoes of love,
My spirit cheers when I master the madness of the voices I hear,
When I'm clear,
When you're clear,
In the true essence of now,
Unafraid to vocalize the truths of your heart,
The purpose of your reality is sparked,
Your visions are seen, felt, and heard,
As the wisdom of your word,
Your Voice,
Speaks volumes . . .

A LETTER TO YOUR FATHER

Believe it or not, I am very guarded with my feelings. I would much rather not tell anyone what I feel. At times I'm still that shy kid in the classroom, but I have made the decision to practice and work to remember who I am. Over the years I have learned that once habits have settled in, you have to fight off the remnants of old ways. It's a challenge, but it's a challenge that I accept. I want, I need, to wade in the waters of good living.

I want, I need, life to be full of experience.

I want to see my potential and then work to walk in it, achieve it. And I have found that I have grown closer to that goal thru what I've shared here in my story.

Whoever you are in the world. Wherever you live in the world. Whatever your creed or religion may be. Whatever your race may be. Whatever language you speak. Whatever culture you proudly represent. We all have one thing in common. Out of the billions who walk this earth, one of the few facts that we can all collectively agree on is that each of us has a father. We all have that man who united with our mother to bring us into this world. We all have that person who helped provide us with the opportunity to experience life in the physical form. We were all born to two individuals who will forever and always be a part of who we are.

With that said, I extend the invitation for you to contribute your story to this thread of self-empowerment. I challenge you to look within and search your feelings. No matter what your relationship may be with your father. No matter if your connection is good, bad, or ugly, I challenge you. I encourage you to applaud him for his contribution to your life. I encourage you to forgive him for any wrongdoing that may have come your way. I encourage you to forgive yourself for any negative thinking. I encourage you to remember what it is to be human. Know that your father was faced with the same challenges all humans face. Have compassion for the battles he may have lost. Let go of your weights. Take the shackles off of your wings. Brand your heart with love. Forgive and remember to forgive again.

Deal with your emotions so they don't one day deal with you.

For me it wasn't easy getting to that point, but I pray that this story might inspire you, might encourage you to write a letter to your father. Together we will champion our healing. There are those willing to listen if you are willing to speak. So take this time to tell your father how you feel. There are so many conversations that my anger, my guilt, and my lack of confidence held me back from having with my father. For those whose fathers are still living, no matter how hard it may be, take advantage of the time you have 'cause you never know when things will come to an end. For those whose fathers have moved on, know that they are still with you, waiting for you to hear that voice, waiting for you to speak to them. You'll be amazed at the joy you will find. You'll feel better at the lift you'll be able to contribute to your family. Most of us want to see our world in a better condition. I feel and I know that the change we seek begins at home. If we start with ourselves, extend to our families, then our neighbors, then our communities and our cities, we will surely see that change come. But again, the change starts with each of us.

That healing begins with you and you and you and me. Let's heal together.

As you move forward, I leave you with these four steps for healing and writing:

1. **Slow Down:** We move so fast thru life. We get caught up in the pace of living, and we forget to take a moment to assess where we are and to visualize where we want to go. Thoughts fire off, and we react. The goal is slowing down and taking the time to meditate, breathe, and focus on who you are and where you want to go. Find your quiet space. Relax. Slow down your mind.

2. **Get It Out:** Pick up a pen, pull out some paper, sit down, and get it out. Hear what your heart and soul are saying. Write down your feelings. Relieve the pressure that your emotions build up. Let go of the pain. Release. Make space. Detox your spirit. Cleanse your self of your emotional waste so you can fill up on what's to come. There's nutrition in your ability to tell your story. There's strength found in reading what's been written. There's new life found in your ability to love without interruption. And it starts with two simple words: *Dear Father.*

3. **Love What's Revealed:** Embrace your truth. Accept what is and what isn't. Don't be afraid of who you are. Embrace the skin you're in. Escape the confusion of your enigmas. Fall in love with yourself and your story. Be happy with the ups and the downs that have shaped you. Everything does happen for a reason. Don't run from your truths. Don't hide from your imperfections. You are imperfectly perfect. Your path has been designed for you to learn and pick up tools for the next chapters.

4. **Activate:** Take action. You're not here forever. Use what you have learned about yourself and move forward. Without fear, without doubt, with your heart filled with love and positivity for yourself and others, take control of your destiny; go hard, believe in your abilities, and thrust ahead knowing that each and every day is a new chance to start again. Work on your dreams. Remember your future. Remember to smile. Remember to laugh. Remember to help and love yourself so you can help and love the next. Remember who you are and choose to be happy.

Dreams Don't Come True, They Are True.

Much love!

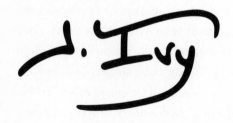

ACKNOWLEDGMENTS

First I have to thank God for all the beautiful blessings, grace, and undying love that you have bestowed upon my family and me. I thank you for my gifts, for the experiences, for the opportunities, for the breath in my lungs, and for the beautiful family you assigned me to. I love you!!

A special thank you goes out to Emily Han, Richard Cohn, Judith Curr, Henry Covey, and the Beyond Words, Atria Books, and Simon & Schuster Family. Thanks for all the effort you have put into this work that I have been looking forward to the world hearing. Thank you for seeing the vision and getting behind this message of healing. I truly know and believe we will change and inspire a lot of lives. This experience has been nothing less than amazing. You all are the best! Like Tarrey says, you all are Beyond Cool!

I want to thank my father, Dad, Jim Richards. In my heart of hearts I thank you for being there, protecting the family and me. I thank you for being inspired to help bring me in to this world. You truly are my guardian angel, and I am thankful that I was blessed with the ability to hear such a beautiful spirit. Your fight, your creativity, your light shines bright and I am amazed at your ability to still shine thru. All I ever wanted to do is to make you and Ma proud.

Ma, what can I say . . . you are the best of the best! Thank you for being the best mother a young cat from the Chi could ever ask for. I truly appreciate your love, your honesty, your wisdom, your smile, your laugh, your concern, your strength, and your creativity. You have sacrificed so much in your life for Virgil, Sergio, and me. That dedication doesn't go unnoticed. I appreciate you so much. You are the truth. You are my angel. (Lacy, thanks for keeping my moms happy!)

Tarrey Torae! So many people have supported us. So many people tried to question us, but our truth and our love for one another hasn't allowed the traps of the wilderness to divide us. You are my heart, my muse, my stagemate, my best friend, my joy, and my smile in the midst of the storm. I thank you for being you, unapologetic, sweet, sincere, passionate, innovative, hardworking, gifted, and talented beyond belief. You have been the greatest gift God has ever given me, the smartest person I've ever known. I look forward to continuing to build our family together. Sing, baby, SING!

To my brothers, Virgil and Sergio, I thank y'all for your strength, your heart, and your light. I've learned so much from you both, and I thank you for being those I know I can call on. I love y'all! I'm proud to call y'all my brothers.

I want to send love and appreciation to my family: Edward and Julia Johnson (love you two . . . rest in peace!); my aunts and uncles and their families, Christine (thank you so much for your love, strength, and reflection) and Charles Kimbrough, Ron and Cheryl Johnson, and Granville and Porshia Porter; Shaneshia Bailey; Sheila and Paul; Cleo and Julia Jamison (Julia, thank you so much for that invaluable lesson of forgiveness) and family; the French family; David and Patricia Nalls and family (y'all are so loved and appreciated and are the nicest people I've *ever* met!); John (rest in peace) and Juanita Harris and family (keep smiling, Nita!); Cedric, Cynthia, and Jonathan Richardson; the Richardson family; the Johnson family; much love to all my cousins, Gloria Elaine Burr, Cuz Larry, Aaron Richardson (producer of "Dear Father" cuz you're the best), Julia Bradley; the Donelson family; the Green family; the Bell Family; and the Washington family.

A special thanks goes out to those who extended their kind endorsements: John Legend, continue shining bright, bruh . . . your music and vision are beyond inspiring. Deepak Chopra, thank you for your wisdom and encouraging words of healing, and a big shout out to the Chopra Family and my sisters Carolyn Rangel and Felicia Rangel . . . *much love!* Sway Calloway, one of the coolest people I've met on my adventure. Thank you for your contribution to our culture. Doug E Fresh, the world's greatest entertainer, you inspired me when I was a shorty. You inspire me now. I appreciate your guidance and genuineness. Estelle, gifted and sweet from the start, thanks for the love and inspiration! Talib Kweli, you've always been a defender of truth and one of the best ever at expressing it. You have been and always will be a brother and friend to our family. Israel Idonije—Izzy! The work you do with the youth around the world means more than any battle on the field. Thanks for caring and inspiring so many. *Bear down!* And to my big brother and mentor Abiodun Oyewole of the legendary Last Poets—over the years you and your brothers have done so much for the culture, the community, and the world. You have inspired so many to reach so far. Thanks for taking me and so many under your wing. You are truly loved.

A very special thanks goes out to Paula Argue. Thank you so much for pointing out an invaluable gift that I had yet to discover . . . I am forever grateful that you made me (excuse me, *encouraged* me) to get on that stage. All jokes aside, you helped save my life. I love you much!!

To André Wright Jr. and family, thanks for yet another dope cover shot; George Stein, thanks for all of your wisdom; and Gary Jansen, thanks for your inspiring words and thoughts. Coodie Simmons, Chike Ozah, Chris Velona, Los Angeles' The Last Book Store and Mike Marasco; Cam Be, Jamaar J, and Erin Hinton: thank you for adding your amazing artistry to this book. There's nothing like working with directors who get it. Your vision is priceless. A very special thank you goes out to Rich Sancho (producer of "Dream Big"), Hector Delgado, Darren Williams, Yasmine Richards, Josh Senior and team, Eddie Rozay, Collin Jordan, Kyra Phillips, Carolyn Disbrown, Olivia Beer, The Points of Light team, and the Service Works Team. Much love to all my guys in Chicago and the South suburbs: Todd Whitaker and family; Jason King and family; Theo Fowler and family; Mike Miller and family; Ryan Yarbrough and family; the Cross, Price, Nance, Nuckolls, Sharkey, Archer, Baron, and Whitehead families; Afrika and the Porter family; Lewis Williams and family; Howard White and family; Emmit Martin; Michelle Wernick; Kurt Williamson; Warren Oliver; Nicole Parrish; Traceye Smith; Kamilah Forbes; Sammy Silver; Melda Potts; Nia Fairweather; Gil Scott-Heron; Dolores Robinson; Chairman Fred Hampton Jr.; Dave Chappelle (thank you for all your inspiration. Your words, humor, and intellect always lift me up. "I need to write!"); Marcus Gradney; Ernie Barnes (Rest in peace brother. Your contributions to life, art, and my own life will never be forgotten.); Bernie Barnes; Luz Rodriguez; Craig Swift; Billy Burke; Greg Magers; Graham Burris; Clive Srail and the Born Fly Clothing family; Molaundo Jones; Brook Stephenson; Marilyn Schlitz; Stan Lathan; Russell Simmons; Bruce George; Sumayya Muhammad and family; Chad and Sylvia Jordan; Saudia Davis; Mobolaji Akintunde; Kalvin Franklin; Mario Fefee; Carl West; Toure Muhammad and family; the Fellowship

Missionary Baptist Church family; the First Corinthian Baptist Church family; the Burrell Communications family; the Commonground Marketing family; the Leo Burnett family; Chicago Public Schools; Chicago radio WVON, WGCI, V103, Power 92, Mario Smith and WHPK; Munson Steed and *Rolling Out* magazine; the *Huffington Post*; Dan Ulsan, JP Anderso, and *Michigan Avenue Magazine*; Maria Davis and family, Andrew Barber; *fakeshoredrive.com*; *gowherehiphop.com*; *rubyhornet.com*; all the blogs that show love; my Rich Central family; my Illinois State family; my University of Illinois family; Ms. Evans; my West Point family; my Lexington family; my Nashville family; my LA family; my New York family; my Harlem family; Judy Smith; the Sylvia's Restaurant family; my Brooklyn Family; the Innovative Artist family; all the universities and colleges that have invited me to their campuses; everyone who has clapped, cheered, and supported me over the years; all the artists I've been inspired by; all the artists I've collaborated with over the years; the mighty culture we call hip-hop and the inspiration you daily produce; to my Rituals family and all the poetry spots that keep the art thriving; and all the poets past, present, and future who toss fear to the side, pick up a pen and a pad, inspire, motivate, create change, save lives, and exercise the most beautiful art in the world: the power of the word.

Last but certainly not least, thank you to my sweet city of Chicago (and the burbs), the *best* city in the world! I thank you for the values, the flavor, the culture, the innovation, the style, the creativity, the work ethic, the go-get-it mentality, and the confidence you have instilled in me. I refuse to believe in the hate that some try to paint us with. I refuse to believe in the hate that we sometimes paint ourselves with. It is time to revert to the love that was instilled in us. Let's stop the killings. Let's build and keep living. I love you more than you'll ever know. Big shout out to Mississippi! Love y'all!!

...UP EARLY FOR SATURDAY MORNING CARTOONS. STAYED UP ALL NIGHT CHRISTMAS EVE WAITING ON SANTA CLAUS. LOVED MONOPOLY, BUT IT TOOK TOO LONG. BESIDES THE ...JUST CAME OUT AND I KEPT *Indiana Jones to* STAR WARS ON REPEAT. BECAUSE I WAS A JEDI WHO WAS SCARED *THUNDER to* GREMLINS WHEN IT FIRST CAME OUT. BUT I WAS BILL *NIGHTMARES WHEN POLTERGEIST.* BY TIME MICHAEL JACKSON CAME OUT, ALIVE *MOONWALKING, FELLING* BY TIME THE WIZ CAME ON. I WOULDN'T TAKE BOTH MONTHS WHEN JAWS CAME ON. AND WHEN WE GOT MODERN 64 WE KEPT THE GAME ON. WE KEPT OUR SETTE TAPES READY TO RECORD WHEN THE RADIO CAME BECAUSE THEY JUST MIGHT PLAY YOUR FAVORITE SONG. TOOK LONG TRIPS TO DISNEY WORLD. SCREAMED OUR BRAINS ON SPACE MOUNTAIN. WAS AMAZED BY THE FOUNTAIN THAT

MICH...

SING RABBITS AND BLUE RACERS. EATING BLUE MOON ICE EAM AND SHERBERT. THEN IT WAS BACK TO THE CITY ...E CATS WERE GETTING SHOT FOR THEIR STARTER ...S AND JORDANS BECAUSE JORDAN WAS KILLING. ...LLING UP THE BASKET AND HIGHLIGHT REEL. WALTER ...TON DANCED AROUND OR RAN OVER OPPONENTS ON THE ...ELD. SO WE IMITATED HIM WHEN MA WOULD MAKE US GO OUTSIDE ...N WE WERE INSIDE I ATE KOOL-AID AND CRACKERS. *GOVERNMENT CHEESE* ...SANDWICHES. IT WASN'T PUNISHMENT, BUT IT FELT LIKE WHEN WE HAD TO STAND IN LINE FOR THE POWDERED MILK ...D GOVERNMENT CHEESE. BUT THAT CHEESE MADE THE BEST ...LLED CHEESE SANDWICHES. WHICH WAS MUCH BETTER THAN ...T BEANS AND RICE MA WOULD MAKE *IN THE CROCKPOT* WHEN WE'RE OUT OF ...MBURGERS AND SPAGHETTI. (BACK BEFORE MY MAMA ...S VEGETARIAN). AND I STILL REMEMBER THE 1ST TIME VIRGIL

Circa 1941. My grandparents, uncle, aunt, and dad. *From left to right*:
Isaac Richardson Sr., Isaac Richardson Jr., Laura Rose Richardson,
James Ivy Richardson Sr., Lillie Christine (Richardson) Kimbrough.

Circa 1970. Jim Richards, aka Dr. Love, and friends.

Circa 1970. My moms, Pamela (Johnson) Richardson.

Circa 1975, Jim Richards WMPP Radio flyer.

Circa 1983. Jimmy and Sergio at home on the South Side of Chicago.

Circa 1982. Jimmy, Sergio, and Virgil at home
on the South Side of Chicago.

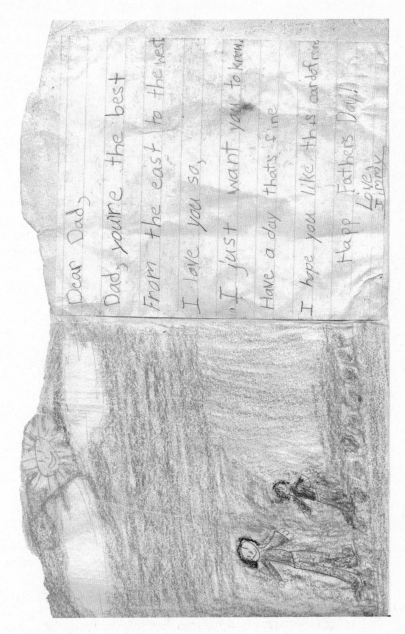

Circa 1982. Father's Day card written and drawn by Jimmy.

Circa 1990. Jimmy at his grandparents' house in the
South suburbs of Chicago.

In Loving Memory

Of

James L. Richardson

SATURDAY, NOVEMBER 20, 1999

Wake ~ 10:00 AM   Funeral ~ 10:30 AM

GOLDEN GATE FUNERAL HOME
2036 West 79th Street
Chicago, Illinois

Reverend L. G. Cook ~ Officiating

Dad's obituary, November 20, 1999.

Dear Father

one million letters written, one million hearts healed

P.O. Box 29 Richton Park, IL 60471 • www.DearFatherLetters.com

Mission Statement:
The Dear Father Letter Writing Campaign's mission is to help inspire healing through writing for children and adults who have grown up in fatherless homes, which will in turn help to prevent this hurt and imbalance from being passed on to the next generations.

The Goals of the Letter Writing Campaign:
The goal of the Dear Father Letter Writing Campaign is to help enhance healing and forgiveness through the art of letter writing. Simultaneously, this can help to reconnect families and communities everywhere, where it is deemed healthy and valuable to those involved. The intention of the Dear Father Letter Writing Campaign is to generate one million letters worldwide from program initiative participants. The following are potential objectives that the campaign hopes to achieve:

- Breaking Cycles of Pain
- Self Awareness
- Clarity
- Happiness
- Self Realization
- Understanding the Past
- Confidence
- Self Motivation
- Healing
- Father/Children Reconnections
- Literacy
- Self Esteem
- Forgiveness
- Leadership

Points of Action:
- Dear Father Letter Writing Campaign
- Dear Dad Dialogues (Group Discussions)
- Community Service Partnerships for Counseling & Personal Development

Call to Action:
- Write a "Dear Father" Letter and submit it to our One Million Letter Campaign
- Become a host for a Dear Dad Dialogue in one of the 25 cities
- Sign up for the monthly online chat on the website www.DearFatherLetters.com
- Attend a book signing and/or Dear Dad Dialogue
- Connect with the effort of Dear Father Letters on social media
- Donate to the cause
- Become a tour sponsor
- Join a local community effort for mentorship and leadership training